HOOPED DREAMS

HOOPED DREAMS

BILLIONAIRES, QPR AND THE PREMIERSHIP PROMISED LAND

MICK KELLY

First published in paperback 2009
by Pennant Books

British Library Cataloguing-in-Publication Data:
A catalogue record for this book is available on request from
The British Library

ISBN 978-1-906015-39-8

Design & Typeset by Envy Design Ltd

Printed in the UK by
CPI William Clowes Beccles NR34 7TL

Pennant Books
PO Box 5675
London W1A 3FB

www.pennantbooks.com

To Andrea, Calum, Finn and Erin

ACKNOWLEDGEMENTS

Many people have helped make this book possible. Huge thanks to:

Rodney Marsh for writing the foreword.

Amit Bhatia, Gianni Paladini, Gareth Ainsworth, Lee Cook, Rodney Marsh, Stan Bowles, Marc Bircham, Simon Barker, Robert Elms, Michael Nyman, Alan Johnson, Graham Poll, Michal McSperrin-Kossak, Howard Prosser, Pete Davies, Mayur Tailor and Dave Thomas for freely giving up their valuable time for lengthy interviews.

Simon Skinner at *QPRnet.com*, for his ever-entertaining football reports.

My mates on *The Times*, Ron Lewis and Pete Lansley, for being top blokes.

Paul Morrissey at QPR for his willingness to help.

Colin Melville for helping me to come up with the initial front-cover idea.

My dad and brother for being my constant companions at games throughout this – and every other – season.

And last but not least, my wife Andrea – for her proof-reading expertise and supporting me through the weekends and late nights devoured by this book.

MICK KELLY
Hoopeddreams@aol.com

FOREWORD

WHAT IS IT that makes us love a football team? Why do we get so high and so low purely dependant on a dodgy offside call, a penalty that should never have been given or our centre forward missing from six yards out?

I love football. I will always love football. Sometimes the heartache of losing against a team like Chelsea saps the emotional batteries more than the exultation from a huge away win against Mansfield, but I still love it. Like everybody else, I can't do without it. It's almost a narcotic.

Over the years no team has taken me to these extremes more than the 'Super Hoops', who will always be *my* team. Right from the start, my love affair with the QPR fans was totally unique. There was the 'Rodn-eee' chant; my 44 goals in a single season; the journey we made from the old third division to the first, winning our only trophy along the way; and then I became the first third-division Rangers player to be capped by England. All through this we enjoyed the support of our loyal fans, all the way.

Today, I am more excited about the club than I've been in a very long time. If you are too, then just open these pages, sit back and enjoy the rollercoaster ride that is the modern Queens Park Rangers Football Club.

RODNEY MARSH

INTRODUCTION

THE SUPPORT OF a football team is a bond between individuals. In the case of my family, the love of Queens Parks Rangers FC is as much a part of the framework of our lives as remembering birthdays and gathering together at Christmas. For my father, my brother and myself, Loftus Road is where we catch up on the family news, have a laugh over a pint and let off some steam. The club has been an essential part of my life for as long as I can remember.

My first clear memory of going to a match is when QPR were playing in the old Division Two. It was 1973, the season the club was promoted, and I was seven. Swindon Town were the opposition, swept aside 5-0 on the day by a team destined for the top flight, with a hat-trick from Stan Bowles and one each from Gerry Francis and Don Givens. They were three players who would become part of the folklore of the club, forming part of the backbone of the side that so nearly won the Division One title just three years later.

I lived on the White City Estate, literally a stone's throw from the ground, until I was five, when my family moved to Trellick Tower in North Kensington, a 30-floor tower block that achieved almost iconic status via its frequent appearances in pop videos and advertising campaigns with an urban edge. This part of west London was solid Rangers during my youth; yeah, you might have found the odd Chelsea fan, but they were few and far between.

The 10-minute tube journey from Westbourne Park to Shepherds Bush always saw a steady stream of Rangers fans getting onboard, and the march down Uxbridge Road afterwards always brought a thrilling sense of belonging as we headed for the stadium.

QPR was recognised as one of London's top clubs back then, with legendary entertainers like Rodney Marsh and Stan Bowles setting the benchmark for what the fans wanted to see on the pitch. And the club's fans had a strong geographical link to the area around Loftus Road.

Rarely did you live on the other side of London and just happen to support QPR. More often than not you did so because you were brought up in west London, or because your father or grandfather was, and this resulted in a passionate, close-knit bond between club and supporters. I would argue that, after what the club has been through over the last decade, you'd be hard-pushed to find a stronger emotional connection between any other London team and its fans.

The financial turmoil and the languishing in the lower divisions have been incredibly painful, and yet sometimes the dark clouds have lifted. The memory of that night in 2003 when QPR beat Oldham in the play-off semi-final will live on for many years to come. Everyone present at Loftus Road was touched by the magic of the occasion, feeling that they were part of something truly special. When Paul Furlong scored, pure joy reverberated around the stadium; the pain of the recent past made success that night all the sweeter.

After the catalogue of problems off the pitch, there was a tangible sense of relief when it was announced that Flavio Briatore and Bernie Ecclestone had stepped in to buy the club in 2007, saving it from an unbearable second period of administration. Lord knows what would have happened if they hadn't.

So, if only for that reason alone, I will always be grateful to Messrs Briatore and Ecclestone. It may sound a bit overdramatic, but I'm just thankful that the club still exists to pass down to my two sons, in the same way that my father passed it down to me and my brother. I'm glad that QPR can still be part of the framework of my family.

The takeover has allowed R's fans to dream again and so, in writing this book, I have set myself certain goals. Firstly, *Hooped Dreams* documents the era of the new owners, concentrating on the 2008-09 season. I've tried to be balanced and objective about a period that began by offering so much hope, and yet stirred so many diverse and conflicting opinions along the way. At times, it felt as if the story of that season was being told as much in the gossip columns of the tabloids' sports pages as on the pitch itself.

Secondly, I've sought the views of fans, both the famous and those not so well-known outside of the confines of the Springbok pub, Q Block or the Upper Loft, giving them a voice to describe this fascinating period in the club's history.

Thirdly, as the club looks forward to a brighter future, I've reflected on the glory years of the past and its heroes from the various eras. For it's important to remember that QPR is a club with a rich heritage; comparisons with what has gone before are always revealing.

Hooped Dreams begins with the takeover and the reasons for it, then records everything that subsequently unfolded via interviews conducted throughout the 2008-09 season. Each interview reflects and analyses what is happening at that exact moment in the campaign, with no knowledge of the drama and controversy that may lie just around the corner.

As the season began, the club had the potential for success both on and off the pitch that had seemed unimaginable just two years before. But would it be realised? And, if so, at what cost to the special bond that existed between the fans and the club?

Would Rangers fans fulfil their dreams and enter the Premiership elite? Or would they end up believing that they had lost possession of their club?

CHAPTER ONE

AS THE OPENING game approached, it certainly felt different. The eagerly-anticipated 2008-09 season possessed a must-see quality that had caught the imagination of Rangers fans everywhere.

The hype in the football media over the summer, combined with that generated by the fans themselves, had created an atmosphere that Loftus Road hadn't experienced for more than 30 years, since the heady days of Stan Bowles, Gerry Francis and Dave Thomas. Back then, they were considered the most skilful and entertaining team in the land.

The ground even looked different that season. There was the big screen above the School End, blue-chip companies on the advertising hoardings – Texaco, Gulf Air, Santander and Lotto – while in South Africa Road the landmark Springbok pub was transformed. Gone were the rough-at-the-edges, Wild-West saloon-bar trappings; in their place was the smell of fresh new paint, bouncers on the door and a 'QPR Fans Only' door policy. "Everyone's smelling the money," said a bloke in the queue at the bar. And everyone within earshot knew exactly what he meant.

An astonishing sequence of events had unfolded at QPR over the previous twelve months and completely redefined the future ambitions of the club. It had resulted in an atmosphere of boundless optimism and expectation.

The new era of Flavio Briatore was about to move up a gear. The flamboyant chairman of QPR Holdings Ltd was also the owner of the F1 Renault motor racing team and a friend of the rich and famous, with a super-cool playboy image that put Austin Powers to shame. (Yeah, baby!)

In the past the gossip columns had linked him with models Naomi Campbell, Eva Herzigova, Adriana Volpe, Elle Macpherson and Heidi Klum, with whom Briatore had a young daughter. As the new season began, however, the stunning woman on his arm in the directors' box was his new wife, the Italian actress and model Elizabetta Gregoraci, 30 years his junior.

When Briatore married former Wonderbra model Gregoraci in June 2008, just a few weeks before the first match of the new season, it was a lavish ceremony attended by a host of celebrities. They were serenaded by pop group Duran Duran, and the star-studded guest list included Formula One supremo Bernie Ecclestone, who had joined Briatore in becoming an owner of QPR, Fabio Capello, England's football coach, Marcello Lippi, Italy's former World Cup coach, Italian Prime Minister Silvio Berlusconi, former Spanish Prime Minister Jose Maria Aznar and Renault F1 star Fernando Alonso.

The Italian media described the event as the 'wedding of the year', as 58-year-old Briatore tied the knot with Gregoraci, 28, at the Santo Spirito in Sassia Church, near the Vatican in Rome. Alonso then drove the newly-married couple to their extravagant reception at the Castello di Torcrescenza. It was reported that the wedding cost two million euros.

Elisabetta's white gold wedding ring, thought to be worth £18,000 and designed by exclusive jeweller De Grisogono, attracted a lot of attention. So did their extended honeymoon, with pictures of the pair relaxing on a Sardinian beach appearing in the British tabloids. Gregoraci had plenty of opportunity to show off her stunning figure in a series of eye-catching bikinis.

But on Saturday afternoons, Gregoraci had to share her man with another lover. Briatore's affair with QPR had begun in August 2007, when Rangers were on the brink of financial disaster. Rangers were sinking into oblivion; relegation, and possibly even liquidation, loomed large at Loftus Road.

Gianni Paladini, the chairman before the takeover, stated he had no idea what would have happened to the club if Briatore hadn't expressed an interest in investing. It was just hours from going into administration for a second time when Briatore stepped in.

The story doing the rounds in west London as the new season began was that the multimillionaire learnt about the possibility of buying QPR completely by accident. He was discussing opening a classy, high-end pizzeria in London when he was contacted out of the blue about the possibility of investing in Rangers. Still thinking about the food business at the time, he initially believed QPR was the name of a barbecue restaurant. But when he finally realised he had a chance to take control of a football club – one in the doldrums, admittedly, but with the huge potential to rise again – it offered him plenty of food for thought. (So the story goes anyway.)

Briatore's record in business is well documented. Having worked as a ski instructor and a restaurant manager in the sixties, a stint on the Italian Stock Exchange had provided his first meeting with Luciano Benetton, founder of the Benetton clothing company. The two became friends and, eventually, business partners.

In 1979, Benetton opened his first five stores in the USA and named Briatore as director of the group's business interests in the States. 10 years later the number of stores in the USA soared to

800, and Briatore became a wealthy man through negotiating the franchise agreements. Benetton was also known for its controversially attention-grabbing advertisements during this period, a calculated campaign which Briatore knew would get everyone talking about his brand.

But, as the eighties came to an end, a new challenge awaited Briatore in the industry of sport. He moved into motor racing and took over the Benetton F1 team in 1989, transforming them from also-rans into world champions within five years, building the team's success around a promising young German driver called Michael Schumacher, who he discovered in 1991.

In 2000 Renault announced its plans to return to Formula One with the purchase of the Benetton F1 team. Briatore was installed as managing director and team principal; his reputation for nurturing raw talent was enhanced further when he discovered Spanish teenager Fernando Alonso in 1999. As his manager, Briatore secured him a race drive with Minardi in 2001 and promoted him to test driver for Renault in 2002.

In 2003 Briatore replaced race driver Jenson Button with Alonso, telling doubters to judge him by results. Renault won both the drivers' and constructors' championships in 2005 and 2006. Briatore also developed a number of business interests outside of sport. He created the Billionaire clothing brand in 1998 and opened a club in Sardinia under that name. He also opened Cipriani's restaurant in Mayfair in 2004 and built up the pharmaceuticals company Pierrel, while operating a Tuscan beach club and a holiday resort in Kenya as well.

But now the plan was to pull off a similar transformation at QPR to those achieved at Benetton and Renault. During the summer of 2008 he told *Marketing Week*: "In F1 there is a large team behind a product – the car. It is the same at QPR, the team. The football is only the product. In sport, business efficiency is everything. If I'm going to invest in champagne, I'll go to France. If I decide to invest in ham, then I'll go to Parma. If you're going to be in football, you have to be in England. And football is treated like a business here."

Briatore made his position perfectly clear: "The first thing to remember is that without us, there was no QPR. It's as simple as that. I don't want everybody telling me what I need to be doing. People believe the club is owned by the fans but it's only a few that put their money down. For the rest of the people, it's easy to criticise [when] they maybe spend £20."

What *would* have become of QPR if he hadn't stepped forward? Paladini paints a picture of unbearable financial turmoil behind the scenes. A second spell in administration would have resulted in at least 10 points being docked under new Football League regulations. But, if the powers that be at the club were to be believed, a far bigger threat also existed: the genuine possibility that QPR may not have come out of administration again.

Paladini stated at the time that the takeover saved the club from liquidation, which by definition would have seen it closed down and its assets divided. It might have been one financial crisis too many for QPR, which had become as much a story off the field as on it in recent years. Would the club have survived another setback? Would Loftus Road have had to be sold? Would Rangers have ended up playing AFC Wimbledon in non-league football?

Paladini portrayed Briatore, reported to be worth around £70 million during the takeover, as a kind of silver-haired superhero. Just as superheroes often come in pairs (or dynamic duos), so Briatore had his own wingman in Bernie Ecclestone, said to be worth about £2.2 billion.

The Formula One supremo had been linked in various ways to the 'Big Four' of the Premiership in the past – Chelsea, Arsenal,

Liverpool and Manchester United. But QPR – a club with history that had fallen on hard times, located not far from his London home – appealed to him. There seemed to be plenty of room for the club to grow.

In August 2007, the pair unveiled plans for a £19 million investment in the club. Under the deal, they paid £1m for QPR's shares and £13m towards its huge debts (estimates of these debts varied from £17m to £21m). The pair also loaned the club £5m, partly to buy new players.

But there was one final piece of this financial jigsaw which needed to be put into place before everything could properly move forward. In December 2007, while QPR lay anchored to the bottom of the Championship, the family of the fourth richest man in the world, Indian steel magnate Lakshmi Mittal, took a 20-per cent stake in the club.

Mittal's family were the richest residents in the UK, worth somewhere in the staggering region of £27.7 billion at the time, considerably more than the £11.7bn fortune of Chelsea owner Roman Abramovich, who came second behind Mittal in the definitive *Sunday Times* Rich List for 2008.

The wedding of Mittal's daughter, Vanisha, to Amit Bhatia in June 2004 was reported to be the most expensive in history, putting even Briatore's nuptials in the shade and costing a cool £30m. In the same year, Mittal also spent £57m buying a luxury mansion in exclusive Kensington Palace Gardens, central London, from a certain Bernie Ecclestone.

To confirm the family's commitment to the club, Bhatia was made vice-chairman of QPR Holdings Ltd, second in command to Briatore. The media declared that QPR had now become the richest football club in the world (on paper anyway).

In March 2008, Briatore and Bhatia, chairman and vice-chairman of QPR Holdings Ltd respectively, sat together to unveil a five-year kit deal with Italian sportswear company Lotto, which would be worth £20m if Rangers were promoted to the Premiership. It was one of the most lucrative sponsorship deals in the history of the Championship, and Rangers' biggest-ever commercial deal. But Briatore told a press conference, "It is completely wrong to compare us to Chelsea. We will not throw our money away. Even though the shareholders are wealthy, it doesn't mean the club is. We want to put the club together in the right way."

Just a week later Amit Bhatia spoke to London's *Evening Standard*, to expand further on he and his father-in-law's plans for the club. He rammed home the same message: "We are nothing like Chelsea and we will not lose control over spending. The expenses involved with QPR are far smaller. The £20m deal [with Lotto] will go a long way to making us profitable, as would promotion."

He stressed that their plans did not include moving ground – for the time being anyway. "One of the most attractive things about this club is the stadium," he said. "So we have no desire to move from here at all. If the day came when a move was warranted – and I guess that was when the results were great, we get promoted and we need a 35,000-seater stadium – then, yes, maybe we'd explore it. But we don't need it today.

"Shareholders should not determine what a club looks like. QPR has a great history and a great tradition and for us to maintain that is of prime importance." Speaking of the club's ambitions on the pitch, Bhatia told the *Standard*, "We started off by setting a three-year target for promotion. If we didn't get promoted in three years, I don't think it would be a failure. We would be disappointed, of course, but I am sure we are going to get there. I don't think any of us has got into this to be second best. We have a specific plan and we will do anything it requires to get the club where we want them to be."

For most R's fans the small details were unimportant. What mattered was that the club seemed to be moving forward, and that a truly miserable era at Loftus Road would be coming to an end. It's easy to forget that Rangers finished fifth in the inaugural season of the Premier League back in 1992-93 – above Chelsea, Arsenal and Liverpool – with Gerry Francis in charge, Les Ferdinand banging in the goals, Andy Sinton tormenting defenders down the flanks and Ray Wilkins pulling the strings in midfield. They finished that season as London's top club.

But QPR's dire financial history is also well known. The club lived the dream after a £10m takeover in 1996 by Chris Wright, the Chrysalis music entrepreneur who had been a Rangers fan for 20 years. He acquired Wasps rugby union club as well, and both clubs played at Loftus Road in a ground-share deal. They were run by a new company called Loftus Road Plc and floated on the stock market. But this period was not a success for the club and, in February 2001, after fans tried to storm the directors' box during a defeat by west London rivals Fulham, Wright stepped down as chairman. He said he'd invested close to £20m into the doomed venture.

Just weeks later, in April 2001, with QPR having lost £27m in about four years, the club went into administration with crippling debts. It was the most spectacular failure among the host of football clubs who entered the stock market in 1996-97.

A month later Rangers were relegated to what was then the second division. They were threatened with expulsion altogether by the Football League in 2002, having been in administration for a year, and escaped only with the help of a £10m loan from the Panama-registered ABC Corporation, acquired at 10 per cent – or £1m – annual interest. This loan was secured against Loftus Road and would become a huge burden to the club during the years to come.

It was understood that £3.5m of that £10m sum was needed to pay back Chris Wright. The remaining £6.5m covered administration and other fees, as well as funds of around £3m to run QPR on a day-to-day basis.

The club didn't need help so much as a kind of divine intervention. Even the Moonie religious cult had enquired about investing in it at one stage. So Briatore's words as he took control offered fans fresh hope: "We are fully aware of the history of QPR and the loyal fanbase that it has, we are therefore totally committed to bringing future success to the club. Gianni, Bernie and I are determined to see the club return to the Premiership within the next four years."

These words went down a storm with fans long starved of success and living in the shadows of their west London neighbours, Roman Abramovich's Chelsea and Mohamed Al Fayed's Fulham. For Gianni Paladini in particular, it was the end of a long and traumatic journey that had seen him allegedly held at gunpoint, ridiculed by fans and risking everything he owned. But now he felt vindicated.

"QPR is my life," he said. "It means more to me than anything else. I live it day and night, 24 hours a day, more now than before. I've had to stick to what I believe in, stay loyal to my principles, and I've met some lovely people through QPR who've helped me get through the most difficult of times. We're now incredibly lucky that we've got these people – Flavio, Bernie and Mittal - in control of the club. Right now is a very exciting time for the club and myself, but we have to make things happen. These people are winners and they don't accept anything but the best."

Paladini didn't share the glamorous world of Formula One with Briatore and Ecclestone, nor did he enjoy the mind-bogglingly wealthy trappings of Mittal's lavish lifestyle. But his life could never be described as dull. He was once a promising young footballer, who had to retire at 18 after breaking his kneecap before playing a single game for his hometown club of Napoli, in southern Italy. He met his future English wife when he was away on tour with Napoli's youth team and became a football agent at a young age, going on to represent the likes of Fabrizio Ravanelli and Benito Carbone.

He was also a businessman, remortgaging his family home to invest £650,000 into QPR in 2004 for a 22-per cent share. The club had been seeking investors since coming out of administration in 2002.

"Look, when I first came here, the club was a bit of a joke," he acknowledged. "We have to be realistic about it, there's no good pretending it was anything else. The club was going nowhere and it was completely shambolic – a mess. I didn't know it was that bad financially when I got involved, but I came in to help the club when no-one else would. So many people promised they would come in and help financially, and they got a lot of publicity saying they were going to buy the club, but they never came in. So I had to take responsibility for it."

Paladini came to England in the late sixties and settled in Solihull, West Midlands, where he married his wife Olga. QPR wasn't the first football club with which he was linked; in 2003, he looked at investing in Port Vale, who were followed by his son Stephen at the time. Negotiations reached an advanced stage before the deal fell through.

Then he turned his attentions towards west London. He said: "I first fell in love with QPR when I saw a game here. I couldn't believe the fans. They were in a lower division and the place was packed. I thought how can the place be completely packed, and the club be losing money, it must be impossible.

"But listen, I don't blame anybody. I came to QPR of my own accord. The only problem is when I got into the office, and realised how bad the situation was, it was too late for me to get out. I had two choices. One was to say OK, I've lost my money, goodbye, I'm going. Or two, to fight my corner and say I'm not going to lose this money, I'm going to make this happen, I'm going to make this club a financial success.

"If I had walked, the club would have gone bust anyway. I put in £650,000, then more. I had to borrow money. I had to remortgage my house. I sold my mother's house when she died and put that money into the club. I had to do everything I could to keep the club going."

During the years before the takeover, QPR seemed to roll from one crisis to another. But a stunned courtroom would hear allegations that made the off-the-field shenanigans at QPR front-page news across the nation.

On 13 August 2005, when QPR faced Sheffield United for the first Saturday game of the new season at Loftus Road, Paladini arrived with his son Stephen, daughter Kate and grandson Gianluca, who was due to be the club's mascot for the match. But Paladini had no idea of the dramatic events that lay ahead.

Nearly 14,000 people were in the stadium, oblivious to the commotion that was allegedly unfolding behind the scenes. This bizarre sequence of events was revealed at Blackfriars Crown Court nine months later, where it was claimed that Paladini was ambushed at gunpoint in the chief executive's office and forced to write out a resignation letter.

David Williams QC, prosecuting, told the jury: "I don't know whether some of you watch television and see *The Sopranos*. This is like something out of a gangster film. It was against this scenario that Gianni Paladini was forced to write his own letter of resignation. He was shouted at, slapped and punched by the group until he complied.

"He had no means of escape and, terrified for his safety, did as he was told." Mr Williams added: "It wasn't the sort of share or boardroom struggle that you might expect in business papers or newspapers. Quite literally, a gun was produced and possibly another held to the head of Gianni Paladini."

The court was also told that Bill Power, club chairman at the time, was aware that "something untoward" was occurring. He went to find out what was happening but was blocked by a group of men who claimed to be acting "on the chairman's orders".

Power told them, "I am the fucking chairman," but was still not allowed to pass. The court also heard how Paladini – who had been asked to quit his position on the board of directors and surrender his shares – eventually managed to break free from his captors and run screaming away from them.

But, after a trial lasting more than seven weeks, the prosecution case collapsed in court and the matter was never legally resolved. In total, seven men had faced charges of conspiracy to blackmail, false imprisonment and unlicensed possession of firearms, but all denied the charges and were acquitted. Judge Charles Byers told the jury to clear the men after the most important defendant for the prosecution was found not guilty of the charges brought before him.

Once the court case had ended the matter remained surrounded in intrigue, with lots of unanswered questions. The exact reasons behind what happened that day at Loftus Road will probably never be revealed to the public.

But what the court case did make perfectly clear was that QPR was a club in turmoil, and could not be expected to advance on the pitch until all pressing off-pitch matters had been sorted out. On a hanger in his office at Loftus Road, Paladini still had a bullet-proof vest he'd been advised to wear after the incident.

Paladini claimed he could have pursued the matter in a separate court case, but could no longer see the point. "People know what happened that day," he insisted. "Still people said afterwards that I was a liar. That it didn't happen. So the police investigated everything. They had about 50 or 60 witnesses.

"On the night of the incident, I was with the police until 1am in the morning, and my family had to be protected, and that was very upsetting . . . The great thing about the court case is that the police investigated everything about my life, ever since I came to England, and they didn't find a single thing wrong."

Throughout this period, Paladini was dogged by suggestions about his business practices which, he argued, unfairly blackened the names of both him and the club. The *Evening Standard* was forced to publish an apology after he instigated legal proceedings over an article investigating his business affairs. "People were saying that I was working with agents, but they found nothing . . . nothing! Show me one bit of evidence that I did anything wrong by the club. No, there was not a single thing.

"The worst part of it all is that people attacked me personally. My grandson saw some of the things being said about me on the website message boards and he said: 'Why are these people saying these things about you, you're not a bad person?' I invested my time and money into this club, yet I still got abused by people."

Events at boardroom level stayed in the news during the months that followed the court case, and so did Paladini. Far from being scared away from Loftus Road, he took a more hands-on approach in running the business affairs at QPR. Paladini ousted Bill Power to become the new chairman, backed by several friends and fellow investors including Brazilian World Cup-winner Dunga and two Monaco-based companies.

However, Power, a season-ticket holder for more than 20 years, was well-known and well-liked among the fans. He'd grown up on the White City Estate across the road from the QPR stadium; working at first as an electrician, he made his fortune through a successful satellite communication company. Replacing him was never going to be a popular move, but Paladini defended his actions. "We looked at the mess that we were in. I'll be honest with you, I said we can't go on like this, we'll go bust anyway. So I said we've got two choices.

"You take the club over, give us the money and I'm gone, no problem – if that's the best thing for the club, that's fine. Or you go and we take the club over . . . It was simply the case that to move the club forward, you had to put money into the club or it would go bust."

Paladini was joined on the board by a Mr Big among Italian players' agents, Antonio Caliendo. Caliendo was another colourful character who may not have been very well known in Britain at the time, but was involved in headline-grabbing stories in his homeland. He'd been at the heart of one of the most famous transfers in Italian football, when his client Roberto Baggio moved from Fiorentina to Juventus and sparked riots in Florence by fans who didn't want their hero to leave.

When Caliendo became chairman of QPR Holdings Ltd, Paladini said he owed his compatriot a huge debt of gratitude: "Don't forget the major person who stopped the club going bust was Caliendo. Without Caliendo, I wouldn't be talking to you now. The club would have gone into administration again, a long time ago."

With red bills stacking up, Caliendo helped raise £1.7m for the club, which went straight towards paying off debts. "I know Antonio very well," Paladini explained. "I used to be an agent myself so we've done a lot work together. Caliendo loaned the club a considerable amount of money to prevent it from going into administration. And he never saw most of it again."

Paladini, with the support of his allies on the board, now had full control at QPR but still had to solve the financial crisis engulfing the club. "And fortunately, I met Flavio. I spoke with him and it took six months for the deal to be done, it didn't happen just like that. But before him, I spoke to many people. I spoke to Silvio Berlusconi [Italian Prime Minister and owner of AC Milan]. I've spent all my life in football and I went to meet people I know."

Through some contacts he'd met at Serie A giants Juventus, Paladini was invited to a party in March 2007 where he spotted Briatore. This was a chance for him to impress a multimillionaire powerbroker in the world of sport. And, just maybe, he may have found the man to help him save QPR from financial ruin. They got chatting, but Paladini didn't have much time for small talk. As he explained, "While we were talking over a drink, I said, 'Would you be interested in QPR?' But he didn't know what QPR was, he didn't have a clue. And he said, 'I don't know if I'm really interested in a football club.'"

But Paladini didn't give up. He knew the courting of Briatore was going to take time, but he was convinced he'd found his man. "The thing went flat. In the meantime, the Grand Prix season was going on and he was here, there and everywhere, so I had to chase him a little bit. He told me he couldn't be linked with QPR or any other football club because of his responsibilities with [the] Renault [F1 team]. So the whole thing had to be kept very, very quiet."

The sale of star winger and lifelong Rangers fan Lee Cook to Fulham in July 2007 did generate some much-needed cash over the summer. Cook even donated £250,000 – his 10-per cent cut of the £2.5m transfer fee – to Rangers to help steer them through their financial troubles.

Cook had been born in Hammersmith, west London, and grew up in a family of Rangers fans. His granddad used to take him down to Loftus Road because his dad worked on Saturdays; his hero was Roy Wegerle, whose name he bore on his shirt. Later, he watched from the Upper Loft as Les Ferdinand and Trevor Sinclair turned on the style, when QPR was one of London's top clubs.

Lee Cook joined QPR as a player on loan from Watford in December 2002, making his first appearance in the local derby against Brentford just before Christmas and providing a cross for Marc Bircham to score in a 1-1 draw. As Cook says, "Kenny Jacket, who I knew from my Watford days, was now at QPR with Ian Holloway, and he was involved in me coming here.

"After watching me playing in a game behind-closed-doors at Arsenal's training ground, against a team with Seaman, Parlour and Kanu up front, Olly came over to me and said he'd like me to come to Rangers on loan and I just said, 'It would be a dream come true to play for you.' I think the game at Arsenal was on a Saturday morning and I was signing by the Thursday.

"And that first game at Loftus Road against Brentford in front of a packed house was something I'll never forget. I had about 25 tickets for members of my family who came to cheer me on. And the buzz of that day convinced me that this was where I wanted to play football. I was playing alongside other QPR fans like Kevin Gallen. I used to watch him play in the past and really admired him and now we were playing on the same side."

Cook played 13 times for QPR in the 2002-03 season and fans wanted his loan deal to become permanent. Before he became chairman of the club, Rangers fan Bill Power got involved in the fight to keep Cook at Loftus Road, but Watford were not keen to sell.

Lee Cook returned to Vicarage Road and missed out on playing for QPR in the play-off final in 2003 against Cardiff, though he did join the army of 30,000 QPR supporters at the

Millennium Stadium. When his Watford contract was up in 2004, as a lifelong fan he signed for Rangers.

As he says, "QPR was a club that was struggling and couldn't afford the contracts other clubs could offer. It was well known that the finances at QPR at the time were quite unstable. But the history of the club and the pride of the fans, that's what got us through it.

"And before the Fulham move, Gianni Paladini told me he didn't want to sell me. He'd only do it if the money was right to save the club. The fee Fulham eventually paid for me helped the club financially and helped them to sign a couple of players."

But Watford's contract with QPR meant they were entitled to 15 per cent of any future sale of Cook. Adding Cook's own 10-per cent signing-on fee on top would have meant Rangers were 25 per cent down on the deal. "That was wrong because the club needed the money," believed Cook.

"So when I had the meeting with Gianni before I left, I said keep my 10 per cent. I signed the contract for Fulham and moved on." It was a gesture that R's fans appreciated, even allowing for the leap in Cook's wages from £4,000- to £18,000-a-week after his move to the Premiership club. During this second spell with QPR, from 2004 to 2007, he'd made 113 appearances and scored 10 goals.

On the blog at his own website, *www.leecook.co.uk*, he said a heartfelt farewell as he left the club: "Being a QPR fan, it's very difficult to leave this all behind but I hope everyone understands that this is something I have to do. It's hard to explain the feeling you get when you wear the shirt of the football team you have supported all your life. My first game, a full house against Brentford, was such a special day for me and my family, and it's just got better since.

"I hope I've excited and entertained the fans over the past

three years and it's been an absolute honour to play in front of everybody at Loftus Road. I will miss the fans. They have been great to me, and I thank you so much for your support and voting for me as last season´s player of the year. It really was a dream come true."

Paladini said that the Cook sale had helped keep the debtors from the door for a while. He made sure everyone was paid on time, the staff behind the scenes at Loftus Road as well as the players, but the financial troubles weren't just going to disappear. "It was a nightmare. Nobody else was interested in buying the club. I had sleepless nights. I had to keep the taxman and the creditors at bay. And fans have to understand there were no other consortiums who were seriously interested. If you had £2m you couldn't solve the problem at QPR back then, because we probably owed £3m, and so it went on . . . Personally, I couldn't do anything else. I had sold everything I had."

The club's debts – reported to be closer to the region of £20m than £3m – meant it was struggling to meet day-to-day running costs. Even the multimillion-pound sales during the previous 12 months of Danny Shittu to Watford and Dean Parrett to Tottenham, as well as Lee Cook to Fulham, didn't stem the cashflow problems.

In early August, as the 2007-08 season began, rumours were rife that Briatore and his Formula One pal, Ecclestone, were interested in buying QPR. But there would be plenty of bluffs and counterbluffs before the deal was done. Two games into the 2007-08 season, on Tuesday 14 August 2007, QPR faced Leyton Orient in the Carling Cup First Round. The press also revealed that day that two new parties had come to the table with offers for Rangers.

The *Daily Mail* reported: "One is believed to be British-based and the other is made up of foreign interests but it is understood that the Briatore bid is still considered the most 'attractive' by the

Rangers board. Although it has been speculated that a deal with the flamboyant Italian businessman could be completed within days, negotiations are finely poised and no deal has been done. Antonio Caliendo, the chairman of QPR Holdings Ltd, flew into London last night as talks with the various parties stepped up. Privately, the QPR board has set a deadline for the end of the month for any takeover to be completed."

Then, that same evening before the Orient match, in a dramatic turn of events the official QPR website carried a shock announcement that the club was no longer for sale. A statement from Caliendo read: "There have been many rumours spread in the newspapers recently about QPR. The club is not for sale. The club will be making no further comment at this stage."

Panic broke out among Rangers fans. Without the sale to a new buyer, they feared the club would go under.

Mayur Tailor and Pete Davies are two supporters who had built up a strong relationship with Paladini, and created *We Are the Rangers Boys*, a popular independent website for Rangers fans. As Davies says: "After the Orient game, after all the fans had gone, we were the last ones left. The media wanted to talk to Gianni about the sale, or no sale as we thought that night, but he wasn't talking to anyone. However, he did come over to us privately, and spoke for about a minute. He said that he thought the deal had fallen through, that someone on the board wasn't selling, and I thought well, that's it . . . we're going to the wall."

Mayur Tailor adds: "I just remember Gianni's face. He was shocked. He looked like he wanted to cry. He had everything to lose if this didn't work out. He'd invested his homes and his own money into this. And suddenly it seemed that everything he'd worked so hard for was in ruins."

Fans were gripped with uncertainty about what lay ahead, but events had developed a momentum all of their own. The Grand

Prix season was in full swing and, on the motor racing circuit that August, British sports journalists were talking about the QPR situation as well as the chances of Briatore's Renault team gaining a victory on the track. Paladini feared that this constant speculation would affect Briatore and his determination to see the QPR deal through. At this stage, the Renault F1 team had to be seen as his main priority.

As was often the case in big-money deals like this, the exact facts were hard to decipher while negotiations were in progress. But the Italian multimillionaire began to show clear signs that he was prepared to move into ownership of an English football team. On 24 August 2007, at about 8:30am, Radio Five Live's motor racing correspondent announced that Briatore would make a statement from the Turkish Grand Prix in Istanbul later that day about his plans for QPR.

At the same time, a statement appeared on the club's official website: "Following the recent comments in the press, the Board of QPR announces that it is engaged in discussions with a number of parties that may or may not lead to an offer being made for the entire issued share capital of the Company. The Board will advise shareholders of any further significant developments."

Briatore later told the media, "We are talking. We are a bunch of friends together. If it happens I am very happy, if not, I am very happy as well. The history behind the club is great and I pass the stadium every time I go to Oxford by helicopter, so I have become friendly with the stadium.

"The idea is like any other. I opened the Cipriani [restaurant] in London but I am not in the kitchen to cook. I have the people managing it. Formula One is my priority 100 per cent, anything else we are doing in a professional way but as a group of friends – nothing dramatic."

But while Briatore was playing it cool, anyone thumbing through the latest QPR accounts and awaiting his decision would have sweated buckets. During the weeks leading up to Briatore's announcement in Turkey, it was revealed that the club had been forced to take out a new £1.3m loan with the ABC Corporation, in addition to an existing £10m loan which was already crippling the club's finances.

QPR had been served with a winding-up order earlier in the summer over VAT and Inland Revenue debts dating back several years of up to £800,000. The deadline for the £1.3m to be repaid to ABC was 15 August 2007, and the club claimed it was going to repay the amount partly from Lee Cook's transfer fee.

It was also revealed that the original £10m loan-repayment deadline had been brought forward from 2012 to 31 July 2008. If QPR did not repay the loan by this date, ABC would have the option to buy Loftus Road for £10m. And these were just the facts that were leaking out of the club over the summer. Were there any more surprises in store?

In his private moments, Paladini would have known exactly how close the club was to re-entering administration and having at least 10 points automatically deducted under Football League regulations. His fear was that QPR might never recover from such a devastating double blow: administration for a second time and the real possibility of relegation from the Championship.

Paladini tried to explain what impact a points deduction would have on a club battling to keep its head above water. "I said to Flavio, the situation is like this. If you delay and don't buy the club now, then you will have to buy the club in a lower division because that's probably what will happen. It will take years for the club to come back up. Unless you come in and buy the club now, then the club is gone.

"Then we had the meeting with Bernie and I think he felt sorry for me, after all I'd been through and the way I'd been treated. He couldn't believe that I'd run the club with no money, on my own. But I knew what I had to do. I had to get what I needed to secure the future of QPR."

On 30 August 2007 it was announced that the deal was complete. Briatore and Ecclestone had ploughed £19m into the club after six months of delicate negotiations, and its future was now secure. Prospects both on and off the pitch were the brightest they'd been for more than a decade. Paladini declared, "It is a dream come true for all the fans and saves this club from liquidation. Mr Briatore wants to do for QPR what Mohamed Al Fayed has done for Fulham and turn us into a Premier League club."

But there was also a heartbreaking downside to all of this: QPR's brightest young star wouldn't be around to share the club's positive future. Just a few days before the announcement, 18-year-old England youth international Ray Jones had died in a motor accident in east London. Police confirmed Jones was one of three people killed in a collision between a black Volkswagen Golf and a double-decker bus. After his death, the club went into mourning.

The next game was against Southampton on 1 September 2007. Under normal circumstances, fans would have been celebrating the completion of the Briatore deal just 48 hours before. But this was not a day for celebration. Instead, putting the importance of the game into perspective, all the QPR players carried Jones's name on their backs as a moving mark of respect for their former team-mate. The club also decided to retire the number 31 shirt, which had been Jones's number. It was the climax of an incredibly emotional few weeks for everyone connected with QPR – the fans, the players, the owners and the management.

With Briatore and Ecclestone in complete control, Paladini stayed on under the new regime as Sporting Director, which meant he ran the football side of QPR and looked after transfer dealings. "I will die with QPR in my heart," he said. "My dream is to take us up into the Premiership, but if I end in this job today or tomorrow, I will still be here with the fans. I'll be sitting with the fans. I love the fans. Sometimes I have a tear in my eye when we win, I get very emotional. I don't think I love anything like I love QPR. I've been here seven days a week, 24 hours a day, for five years.

"How can you do that and not love your job? I suffer in my own way if we lose. My wife leaves me alone after a game. And I don't look at the papers on a Sunday if we've lost. I'm a very bad loser. How can you be a good loser, you've lost before you start then. If you invest time and money in something, you don't want to be rubbish. If you run a business, whatever it is, you love your business, you love what you do, otherwise why are you doing it?

"I've worked incredibly hard for this business and got, I believe, the three best people for the job together – Mittal, Bernie and Flavio. The club is now safe for many reasons. These people don't fail, they can't be allowed to fail on something like this. They are determined to make this work. I promise you that we are the envy of many clubs. They think we have hit the jackpot."

CHAPTER TWO

WHEN FLAVIO BRIATORE and Bernie Ecclestone signed on the dotted line for a £14m takeover of Queens Park Rangers, the club's future was secure. The threat of administration disappeared and a decade of financial crisis came to an end. The spiral of debt that had engulfed everyone associated with the club was over.

But for the club to make the step up to become a recognised Premiership force – the stated desire of the new owners – further plans needed to be put into motion. Their combined billions were not quite enough to give them the extra financial clout they needed, so they turned to one of the richest and most powerful men on the planet for help.

Lakshmi Mittal is a London-based Indian billionaire industrialist. In March 2008, he was reported to be the fourth wealthiest person in the world, and the single wealthiest of Asian origin, by the respected *Forbes Magazine* – a considerable jump up the rich list from 61st place in 2004. The Mittal family by then owned a controlling majority stake in ArcelorMittal, the world's largest steel company, which produced 110 million tonnes of the industrial metal – about 10 per cent of the world market.

Mittal's house in Kensington was decorated with marble taken from the same quarry that supplied the Taj Mahal, an extravagance which led to his home being dubbed 'Taj Mittal'. *The Financial Times* named Mittal as its 2006 Person of the Year, and in May 2007 he was lauded as one of the 100 Most Influential People by *Time* magazine in the USA.

His influence and impact on the world of commerce was without question, but could he make a similar impact in football? In the past, he had been linked with possible purchases of Premiership sides Wigan and Everton, but hadn't been convinced enough to invest in these propositions. But he would be persuaded to participate in the new era at QPR by his friends Briatore and Ecclestone.

His son-in-law, Amit Bhatia, would become his representative on the board and also QPR's vice-chairman. As London-born Bhatia explains, "I lived in India up until the time I took my A Levels. I was quite a promising cricketer in my youth and came to London in a junior national side, an up-and-coming players' tour. It was a three-month tour playing different county sides. I played against some schools which quite liked me and offered me the opportunity to play in this country on a scholarship.

"I used to come to England a lot because my mother's family has always lived in London. My parents were always very supportive of me playing and I ended up joining Dulwich College in southeast London and played cricket with them for one season."

Bhatia went back to India to finish his schooling when that season came to an end and then headed to Cornell University for four years, an Ivy League university in New York where he studied economics and investment banking. When he completed his studies he moved to London and into the high-risk world of investment banking, where he worked for major banks like Morgan Stanley and Credit Suisse. He eventually set up his own investment and private equity companies, Swordfish Investments and Swordfish Capital Management. Like his father-in-law, he clearly got a buzz out of the cut and thrust of big business deals, but sport also played a major role in both their lives.

As he says, "My family are huge sports fans. My father and my father-in-law love sport. I've travelled to World Cups and been to the Olympic Games. We share our great love of sport by getting involved in different things. We run a trust in India, to help sportsmen and women without the finance to support their sport careers and to inspire them to chase their goals and reach for the highest levels. This is something we feel very passionately about. India had never won a gold medal before the last Olympics, but we achieved one in Beijing with Abhinav Bindra in the air rifle event and we financed his trainer, bought his plane ticket, everything. This was a wonderful achievement for us.

"Before we got involved with QPR we had received enquiries about getting involved with different clubs. Agents offered us opportunities. These offers were for Premiership clubs and we looked at a whole bunch of them. We have a lot of friends who own different clubs and we talked to them too. This was something we looked at closely but nothing tempted us to make a financial commitment. I think you have to be in love with and feel very passionately about a club to want to be involved with it and make a difference."

The necessary momentum was about to be provided. The news of the Briatore-Ecclestone takeover made back-page headlines, catching Bhatia's eye as he left his office in central London one afternoon. "I saw a newspaper headline that Flavio and Bernie had come in and saved QPR, which I found very interesting," he recalls. "My wife had lived in Notting Hill for four or five years, and I had visited Loftus Road to see a bunch of games in the past with some friends. I shot off a text message to Flavio, just saying I'd heard the great news and wished them all the success in the future.

"A couple of days later I got a call from Flavio. He said he wanted to come over and discuss a few things over a coffee. Flavio, my father-in-law and myself sat down and talked for a while, then Flavio said, 'The real reason I'm here is to discuss this opportunity at QPR with you.'

"Other people had mentioned getting involved with football clubs in the past, but the day you get involved you have to feel very strongly about it. It's not just a simple financial investment. So many fans feel so passionately about football and their clubs, you have to be sure you're making the right decision. When Flavio came over, he talked about his vision for the club and the huge potential QPR had. We had a great conversation and then visited a couple more games. We wanted to understand the club and its history.

"We watched the game with the fans, learning as much as we could about the club before we got involved. And we came out of that period thinking here was this great club in central London that had played at the highest level in football in the past, but had also played in divisions below that high level as well. It had a great history and just needed a bit of nurturing to return the club to where it once belonged.

"Bits of the club needed to be fixed. But this was something that really appealed to me – I could really get my teeth into this. Subsequently, we agreed to become involved as shareholders. It was a great opportunity brought to us by Flavio. My family and I thought very strongly about this. We wanted to help the club get back into the Premiership.

"The club was hours away from administration when Flavio and Bernie stepped in to save it. By the time we got involved they'd already saved the club, but there was quite a lot of financial restructuring that still needed to be done. Money had to be spent because loans had to definitely be paid off. In financial terms, the club was in very dire straits. It needed someone to come in and fix it.

"It was a big challenge, but at the same time it offered a wonderful opportunity to get involved. Here was QPR, in its own period of great financial uncertainty, needing to be rescued and built up. There were old debts and bad debts that needed to be got rid of." Briatore's boardroom team was complete and the next chapter in his colourful business career had begun.

For too long Rangers fans had had little to cheer about, as Chelsea chased Champions League success and Fulham established themselves as long-term survivors in the Premiership. But now they could permit themselves some hope, because the poor neighbours were being heralded in the media as the richest football club on the planet.

In Ecclestone and Mittal the club had secured a couple of high-profile billionaires who could hold their own with oligarchs from Moscow to Knightsbridge, plus a flamboyant figurehead in Briatore who had an impressive network of top-drawer contacts across the sporting world. It was these connections that led to far-fetched stories of Luis Figo and Zinedine Zidane arriving at Loftus Road. But would they have signed up for a side in the Championship? Did they even know what it was?

Many doubtless raised a wry smile when they read that Figo had to deny reports he was heading to Loftus Road. The Zidane rumours, linking the greatest player of his generation to a coaching post at Loftus Road, were instantly laughed off by some but given more credence by others. This was how events began to unfold on a headline day in W12.

It was the last game of the 2007-08 season: West Bromwich Albion at home, champions elect of the Coca Cola Championship, who would be presented with the trophy on the pitch at Loftus Road after the match. Just 12 months earlier the prospect of watching this presentation on home turf, of seeing the sheer ecstasy enjoyed by West Brom's fans and players alike, would have sent Rangers supporters into a deep depression. Back then it was an achievement to stay in the Championship and stay in the black, both of which seemed like losing battles.

But one year later, QPR was a club reborn and Loftus Road a stadium full of fresh hopes. The morning of the West Brom game, Sunday tabloid *The People* ran the story that Zidane was being lined up as QPR's player coach for the 2008-09 season. It was the main sports story on everyone's mobile phone as the game kicked off that lunchtime, and the only topic of conversation at halftime. Would Zidane really come to west London? What would happen to the first team coach of that time, Luigi De Canio? Would he stay or would he go? Or would he be head-butted into submission?

After managing a number of the less fashionable Italian clubs – including Pescara, Udinese, Napoli, Genoa and Siena – De Canio had been brought to QPR by Briatore in October 2007. He replaced manager John Gregory, who had his contract terminated, and caretaker manager Mick Harford, who had a brief spell in charge before De Canio's arrival.

De Canio became an instant hit with the fans during his first season at the helm, because he encouraged talented players like Akos Buzsaky and Rowan Vine to play with flair and style. They were playing in a manner Rangers fans had grown accustomed to down the years, and climbing the Championship table to safety.

Along with the new owners, the coach was immortalised in the supporters' song 'Gigi De Canio, Bernie and Flavio', sung to the tune of the classic operatic aria 'La Donne e Mobile'. Made famous in its original form by tenors such as Luciano Pavarotti and Placido Domingo, it was now adopted and adapted by Q Block, the section of the ground from whence most chanting emanated. As a terrace song, it captured perfectly the sense of optimism surrounding Loftus Road during the 2007-08 season.

De Canio had guided QPR to 14th place in the Championship after taking control, with a record of 12 wins, 12 losses and 11 draws in 35 games. But his position as first team coach looked far from secure as his first season in charge drew to a close.

On the day of the West Brom match, some fans were getting caught up in the hype surrounding Flavio's revolution and genuinely thought it possible that Zidane, the French maestro, could be brought in to replace De Canio and perform his magic in W12. The more cynical laughed it off, and there was a sizeable third body of opinion who thought De Canio had earned the right to lead the club for another season.

As the final whistle blew at the end of the West Brom game, which Rangers lost 0-2, thousands of R's fans showed no intention of leaving the stadium. The away fans were singing and hugging as someone hurried out, clutching the Coca Cola Championship trophy. Rangers fans just looked on. They wanted to thank their own team for turning around a horrible start to the season into one full of potential, and knew that Rangers were going to do a lap of the pitch after the trophy presentation.

But they also had another reason for hanging around. They wanted to sample what it was like to be a team of winners again. To be awarded trophies, to gain entry into the Premiership, the most famous and important football league in the world. There was a sense that scenes like this were now within QPR's reach, that their club could be next in the queue.

"Keep the seat warm for us mate, we'll be swapping places with you next season," quipped one grey-haired bloke in the Ellerslie Road stand. Meanwhile, the silver fox on the pitch – in his trademark designer shades, leading the players on their lap of the ground – was probably thinking exactly the same thing, if not expressing it in quite the same way. Briatore was already saying to anyone who would listen that QPR would emulate West Brom and enter the Premiership. The question for him was not if, but when?

And who would be at the helm?

The debate over who was going to lead the players into this new era would be resolved within days, in a way that nobody anticipated. In a shock move, Luigi De Canio moved back to Italy for personal reasons and by mutual consent. It disappointed Briatore, who tried to tempt De Canio by offering him a substantially improved deal. But for reasons De Canio wouldn't publicly divulge, he felt he had to return to his homeland. However, it wasn't Zidane who took his place. It wasn't even another foreign manager.

Iain Dowie was the board's choice as first team coach, and not a hugely popular decision among the fans. As the new campaign approached, all the experts speculated about how mega-rich QPR would fare with Dowie in charge. They all had Rangers listed among the favourites for automatic promotion, and so W12 waited for the new season to begin with bated breath and eager anticipation.

Barnsley at home would be the first match of the 2008-09 season. Would it be a successful launch to the new campaign or another false dawn for R's fans?

CHAPTER THREE

AS AN EXPECTANT crowd took their seats for the Barnsley game, the opening match of the season, there was an electric buzz of excitement in the air. The first game of the season always brought fresh hope and dreams of promotion. But this was different. For the vast majority of the 15,000 fans in the stadium, there was a sense that just about anything seemed possible for this side under the new, mega-rich owners.

For starters, there was the return of a Loftus Road hero. Lee Cook, who transferred to Fulham in 2007, had returned to QPR on loan. In 2008 he'd also been briefly on loan to Charlton, who'd been visitors to W12 in April. The stadium was heaving, and the way he was welcomed back by Rangers fans left a lasting impression on him.

"When Charlton played Rangers at Loftus Road, I just wasn't expecting the reception I received. It blew the roof off. My family was there, it was a full house and it felt like every side of the stadium was singing my name. They were chanting, 'Cookie is a Ranger,' and it was just a shame that I didn't last the whole game."

Sitting in the changing room, after he had to be substituted in the first half due to injury, he thought about the reception he'd received. "It dawned on me how much that meant. If it didn't work out at Fulham, I wanted to come back here."

Cook also met Flavio Briatore and Bernie Ecclestone for the first time that day. He was going down the tunnel after the warm-up when he bumped into Gianni Paladini, who put an arm around him and said, "Meet our new owners."

"Flavio and Bernie had big smiles on their faces and I said nice to meet you," recalls Cook. "But then Charlton manager Phil Parkinson dragged me away because we had a game to prepare for. It was quite a funny experience really."

During the pre-season, before the start of the new 2008-09 campaign, Cook was back at Fulham, hoping to be part of the club's first-team plans for the new Premiership season. But then he got an unexpected call from Fulham's chief executive, who revealed they'd received an offer from QPR to take him on loan for the new season. It had been accepted. QPR was the only club that Cook would have contemplated for another loan spell, so he met Iain Dowie and Gianni Paladini for dinner that evening.

"Iain told me his plans for the club and what he wanted from me and it all sounded very interesting. I was leaving a Premiership club in Fulham but it seemed clear to me that Rangers would be playing Premiership football sooner rather than later. They'd obviously done a lot of work to the ground and they showed me all the boxes and the stadium refurbishment. The new owners were spending some money and in the January window they'd bought some good players.

"There was an aura about the place. This wasn't a QPR side that would be fighting relegation like the last time I was here. There were plans in place to help it grow into a Premiership club and I wanted to be part of that. If I was going to play Premiership football with anyone, I wanted it to be with QPR."

For the first game of the new season, Lee Cook and his latest team-mates took to the pitch alongside their Barnsley opponents to a fanfare of fireworks. There were flamethrowers, cheerleaders hopping around clutching blue pom-poms and the surreal sight of Gulf Air stewardesses waving enormous flags.

Gulf Air was the team's new high-profile shirt sponsor, a record-breaking deal worth £7m over three years provided QPR was promoted to the Premiership, another ambitious off-pitch commercial development under the new regime. The sky was literally the limit. To put this into context: five years previously, JD Sports had paid £37,000 a year to sponsor QPR; before the Gulf Air sponsorship, Birmingham City's £500,000 deal with F&C Investments had been the most lucrative in the second tier of English football.

Vice-chairman Amit Bhatia explains the board's approach: "What we've learnt in football is that the chances of generating enough money to run a club self-sufficiently are very slim. Neither I nor anyone else involved in the club thinks we can make QPR self-sufficient. That's not the idea behind our involvement at all. We've always known this would cost us money.

"We have signed some big-name sponsors for the next few years and they will help us to move forward and raise the profile of the club. They've been prepared to commit long-term and this is a level of sponsorship we didn't have in the past. They're buying into the future success of the club and we're very proud of the calibre of sponsors that we've got on board."

Loftus Road seemed very showbiz this season, capped off by the sight of 'It Girl' Tamara Beckwith sitting alongside Briatore and Ecclestone in the front row of the directors' box at the Barnsley game. As images appeared on the new big screen of Briatore and Ecclestone in the stand, ripples of applause went round the stadium. But the Ellerslie Road stand still had an air of uncertainty as kick-off approached.

"For God's sake, let us score first," said one fan. "This can all go horribly wrong . . ."

"Nah, it will be alright this season," another replied. "This year it's going to be different. We're the richest club in the world mate!"

He had to be right. How could Rangers cock this one up? The bookies had them as second favourites for automatic promotion that morning behind Birmingham City, and when did they ever get it wrong?

"Yeah, you're right mate. Ignore me, flapping as usual. Come on you R's!" shouted the first fan as he sat a bit more comfortably in his seat. But, after the game kicked off, the opening 10 minutes confirmed his initial fears. It was squeaky bum time at Loftus Road . . . again.

John Macken came close for Barnsley after just two minutes, but Radek Cerney gathered. Then, after a couple more chances, Brian Howard directed a defence-splitting pass between centre-back and right-back. £1.2m signing Iain Hume was through on goal and found the back of the net. Five minutes into a new season full of promise and Rangers were one down to a side bookies had picked as relegation candidates. But what did the bookies know anyway? During the next 10 minutes Barnsley could have scored again, Dexter Blackstock clearing off the line.

The defence – or lack of it – became a first-half talking point. All the regulars in the Ellerslie Road Stand had an opinion, most of which were unrepeatable. One of the more constructive comments was that this new-look rearguard needed time to gel. Cerney in goal, signed from Spurs, Peter Ramage, from Newcastle, and Kaspars Gorkss, a Latvian international eventually prised from Blackpool after drawn-out negotiations, all appeared to be shrewd buys during the summer.

But as they lined up alongside Fitz Hall and Damien Delaney, they looked like a last line of defence that could be exposed by

Barnsley almost at will. They looked like exactly what they were – a collection of players who hadn't played together before in a competitive game. Keeper Cerney received the most stick as home fans chanted the name of Lee Camp, the popular keeper he'd replaced in goal.

All eyes were on Iain Dowie in the dugout. Throughout the previous week there had been stories in the press that he'd already fallen out with Briatore after a row and that he was on the brink of the sack, before the season had even begun. This start to his tenure in charge was making the atmosphere decidedly tense, until one of the summer's other signings took the game by the scruff of the neck.

Emmanuel Ledesma – a 20-year-old Argentine secured on a season-long loan from Italian Serie A side Genoa, who no Rangers fan had probably heard of before that summer – was looking like a class act and a smart purchase, running at the Barnsley defence. He almost single-handedly sparked the comeback, flashing in a free-kick that led to a Blackstock shot against the bar that was eventually bundled into the goal by Fitz Hall. Just two minutes later Hall scored again, a volley over his shoulder that looked anything but a centre-half's goal. But the brace seemed to go to Hall's head as Rangers gunned for a third. When Darren Moore brought down Patrick Agyemang for a penalty, Hall stepped forward to take the spot-kick; his hat-trick attempt was awful and easily saved, a more traditional centre-half's effort.

The final score was 2-1, and while the performance was less than convincing against a side not expected to be vying for promotion at the end of the season, one feature did seem encouraging: Ledesma was named man of the match, while Daniel Parejo – a young Spaniard who arrived on loan for the season from football giants Real Madrid with a glowing reputation – came on as substitute. Parejo had been unveiled as a QPR player the previous week; in the Barnsley programme, Iain Dowie's notes were dwarfed by a picture of him and Briatore standing either side of Parejo, showing off his new Number 7 shirt.

Big things were expected of this prodigious young talent, rated highly at Real Madrid's Bernabeu Stadium, and with last season's star performers, Akos Buzsaky and Rowan Vine, sidelined due to an operation and a serious leg fracture respectively, perhaps it would be Ledesma and Parejo who would leave their mark on QPR's bid for promotion.

The club had first refusal to buy Ledesma once the loan season was complete. But the big question mark against him and Parejo at this stage was: could they mix it when the going got tough away at Wolves or Cardiff? Or would they go missing when the studs went flying? Would they impress during the entire season, or fade before Christmas as a grinding Championship campaign took its toll? One thing was certain: they'd made an immediate impact with young fans, captivated by their Latin skills.

A boy who couldn't have been older than 10 was doing his impression of Ledesma for his dad, weaving in and out of passers-by after the match with a pretend ball at his feet. Dowie acknowledged that a new cult hero may have been born, and the Argentine provided him with a helping hand as he overcame the tricky start to his new reign at the club.

After the final whistle, Dowie faced the waiting media in the post-match press conference. He admitted that he was under pressure to succeed at QPR this season, but dismissed out of hand the story that he was nearly sacked after a row with Briatore. As he said, "The people running the club are very high-profile, they have had success wherever they have been, and that pressure comes with the territory.

"All this talk about me has been a load of tosh. You either

embrace it or hide under a stone and ignore it. For me, it's a case of taking it head on and enjoying what I have with a great bunch of players."

He seemed to have got his message across to the football writers loud and clear – for the time being anyway. 'He's Iain Wowie' declared the *News of the World* the next day. For Dowie, it seemed like job done, but with only one down and 45 more games to go.

Iain Dowie was a rare breed, dedicated to the game but with an intelligence that stretched beyond football formations. (He was so clever, in fact, that he'd added a whole new word to the English dictionary – more of which later.) At 16 he was rejected as a player by Southampton, but achieved far more success in the classroom. The old saying that, for most players, skill on the pitch usually came at the expense of exam results off of it was turned on its head by Dowie. He studied for a master's degree in mechanical engineering at the University of Hertfordshire, and went on to work for British Aerospace.

A career as a footballer was not an obvious choice at this stage in his life, but he carried on playing non-league football for Cheshunt FC, in Hertfordshire, where his brother Bob also played. He moved down the road to St Albans City to improve his fitness, then on to Hendon, where he was eventually spotted by Luton Town and got his break in the professional game.

A successful playing career as an old-fashioned, no-nonsense centre forward also took him to West Ham, Southampton, Crystal Palace and finally QPR, as player-manager of QPR's reserve side. It was at Rangers that Dowie first cut his teeth in management, with a brief spell as caretaker-boss in the autumn of 1998, after Ray Harford was dismissed and before Gerry Francis took over. His record was two games, one win and one defeat, a 50-per cent success rate.

A career as a manager always seemed to be on the cards for Dowie. He was offered the job of assistant manager at Oldham Athletic before becoming their fulltime boss. He showed early signs that he had what it took to be a success in the managerial hotseat, leading the club into the Division Two play-offs in the 2002-03 season. But financial troubles rocked Oldham and Dowie lost much of his first-team squad. Times were so tough that he and the remaining Oldham players were not paid for several months.

It was in his next job that Dowie made his name as one of the most exciting young managers in the country at the time. He took control at Crystal Palace in December 2003, who were a lowly 19th in the old Division One and in need of inspiration. Under Dowie's leadership they certainly received it, winning 17 out of 23 games.

He completely transformed the atmosphere and training regime at the club, introducing more discipline, and they sneaked into the play-offs in sixth place. After beating Sunderland on penalties in the semi-final, Palace overcame Dowie's former club West Ham in the final, securing a place in the Premiership and plenty of accolades for their ambitious young boss. His star was rising.

Palace's reign in the top flight would last only one season as they were relegated on the final day, but Dowie continued to impress. He remained at Palace when the club was relegated to the newly-formed Championship, despite rumours linking him with other Premiership clubs. He would leave Palace by 'mutual consent' on 22 May 2006, following discussions with chairman Simon Jordan who was furious when, just eight days later, Premiership club Charlton Athletic announced Dowie as their new boss.

Dowie was famously issued with a writ by Jordan during the press conference that introduced him as the new manager, claiming he had been misled about Dowie's reasons for leaving

Crystal Palace. Jordan said he'd been given assurances that Dowie had left the club to be closer to his family, who still lived in the Northwest, which Dowie strenuously denied.

From this controversial point onwards, his glowing managerial CV lost some of its shine. Dowie replaced the successful Alan Curbishley at Charlton, who proved a hard act to follow. After just 15 games and a disastrous start to the season, Dowie departed from the south London club in November 2006.

Dowie was then named as Coventry City boss in February 2007; after some impressive wins, the Sky Blues would finish the season 17th in the Championship table. Just a year later, however, in February 2008, Dowie would part company from Coventry due to significant differences of opinion between the management team and the board as to how to move the club forward.

In May 2008, QPR appointed Dowie as their new first team coach following the previous week's departure of Luigi De Canio. Dowie said: "I'm privileged to have been given the opportunity under the new ownership to return to the club where I served my managerial apprenticeship. This is a very exciting long-term project. I've been thoroughly impressed by the new investors and their fresh, aggressive and innovative approach to all sporting matters, as well as the marketing and commercial aspect of this football club. QPR is a fantastic club, with a successful history and I'm going to relish the challenge that lies ahead."

Gianni Paladini added: "Iain Dowie has a proven track record in the Championship and we are delighted to have him on board."

He was chosen because the board believed he had the experience to get the club out of the Championship, but he wasn't a universally popular choice. To critics and fans, he wasn't the glamorous appointment they expected for the richest club in the world.

Looking back over the dramatic transition from De Canio to Dowie, Pete Davies of *We Are the Rangers Boys* website said there were no early warning signs about De Canio leaving, despite the tabloid headlines about Zidane before the West Brom game on the last day of the 2007-08 season. In fact, it was believed that De Canio's contract was going to be extended in the summer.

In the QPR programme for the West Brom game, De Canio wrote: "The fans, the players and the owners are so passionate about their football and that is something I will always remember about this season. The whole experience has been so enjoyable and I am already looking forward to the start of the new campaign. A lot of people have asked me what we can expect from QPR next season and while I don't like making predictions, I have great confidence in this group of players."

The week after the West Brom game, Pete Davies and a few other fans had planned to meet De Canio and Paladini for an end-of-season drink at a pub in Hammersmith. "Gianni and Gigi were going to be there to celebrate the end of the season with us," Davies explains. "We had a good relationship with the club and it was going to be the last time we'd see each other until the new season began.

"That Thursday, just four days after the end of the season, rumours started to spread that Gigi had left. The club told us that he had left for personal reasons." The club started interviewing replacements immediately; possible candidates for the vacant post included Sam Allardyce, Steve McLaren, Paul Ince, Steve Cotterill, Darren Ferguson and Dowie. There was one obvious common factor among them: they were all English, while the Italian-speaking De Canio had struggled to master the language.

With all this uncertainty behind the scenes, the last thing Davies and his mates expected was that the planned meeting with De Canio that night would still go ahead. They were amazed when Paladini told them De Canio was still going to turn up for a drink with the fans.

"We all went to the pub on the Thursday after the end of the season and he was brilliant. We couldn't believe he turned up to be honest, but fair play to him, he kept to his word. We did an interview with Gigi for our fans' website which would prove to be the last ever interview with him. The last time he spoke to QPR fans wasn't on the official website, it was through ours, which we're really proud of.

"Everyone was sad that night, even De Canio was sad. In him, we saw someone who played attractive football – from playing crap football, we were now playing the Rangers way, football that was pleasing on the eye. He brought back the old QPR style. He was someone we respected and he'd come to symbolise the attractive way we now played, from rubbish to passing on the floor.

"This was the last chance we'd have to thank him for it. And we were lucky. He can't speak good English, but there was a guy with him who spoke perfect English and Italian, and he translated the interview for us. It was one of those moments I'll never forget."

Through the translator, De Canio expressed his own personal gratitude: "Thank you from the deepest part of my heart. QPR fans are fantastic. They've given me the best time since I've arrived in London. Thank you for the affection you've shown me. You made me feel like one of you, and for that I will remember you for the rest of my life. I'll never forget you. I'm sorry everything has happened very quickly, but one day I will come back and do it [say goodbye] better."

With that, he posed for some photographs and was gone. Davies recalls, "As he left the pub, that poignant moment when he waved back was caught on camera. We were singing De

Canio's name and some of the people there were in tears. But this guy was gone. We loved him. About 7000 people watched that interview on our website. We usually get 1200 or 1500 people watch our weekly features, but 7000 watched that one. That's our highest-ever figure."

After those emotional farewells, Pete Davies's evening took an even more dramatic twist. "When De Canio had gone, our attention turned straight away to who was going to replace him. I got hold of Gianni on the phone and asked, 'Is it right about Dowie?' He wouldn't say yes, but he wouldn't say no. He just said, 'We've spoken to him and he's someone we admire.'

"I was with my mate Funky, and my wife was also there, and I said to Gianni, 'Right, where are you?' He goes, 'I'm in Knightsbridge.' There's a hotel in Knightsbridge with a casino in it, that's where he was. Now, by this time, you've got to remember we've said our farewells to Gigi and we think Dowie's going to get the job. My instant reaction was that we've got to talk Gianni out of this.

"This could just have been a reaction to seeing Gigi leave, plus all the hype over the names that have been linked to the job by this time, Zidane and the like. But I had never gone out with Gianni in the evening before on a one-to-one basis – nor have I since – and that night I felt compelled to go down there and tell Gianni not to take Dowie.

"I said to my mate Funky, who was hardly dressed for a night out in a Knightsbridge casino, 'You're dressed in shorts, so you're coming to my house first to put on a suit. I've bought some new shoes, you're wearing them. I'm size 11, you're size nine, but that doesn't matter, you're wearing them anyway because we're going straight to that casino, where we're going to tell Gianni that he's not going to take on Dowie.' We were very passionately against him. But, at the end of the day, who are we to go and tell a chairman of a football club who to take on and who not to take on? We just felt we had to do something; we've come this far – we've got Flavio and Bernie now . . . and you're giving us Dowie? Surely not . . ."

Later that evening, when Davies confronted Paladini in the casino about De Canio, he noted to his surprise that their former first team coach was at the same venue. When De Canio had left the pub earlier that evening, Davies was convinced it would be the last time he'd ever see him. But, just an hour later, there he was – standing a few feet away, playing roulette. Paladini explained to Davies that the board thought Dowie was the best man to get QPR out of the Championship, and that the players also wanted Dowie. Fitz Hall and Mikele Leigertwood had both played for him in the past, at Oldham and Crystal Palace respectively, and the new board decided that a manager with a proven track record in the Championship was the ideal candidate.

As Paladini says, "The idea was to find somebody who'd already achieved results in this division. Iain Dowie is a good manager and he's a good man. I like him as a human being. I've worked with him and he's the best manager I've ever worked with. The players love him. He's here every day before everyone else at 8 o'clock. He works very hard and he wants to be successful."

Dowie signed a two-year contract. His role of first team coach was based on the much-maligned continental model, of which Paladini was a staunch defender. Dowie would look after matters on the field while Paladini oversaw the purchase of players. As the latter says, "The way we work is really no different to any other club. At the end of the day, he's the manager of the players. It's just that he doesn't have to deal with the agents, with the other clubs or chairmen. He'll just say, 'I want this player or that player,' and I'll try to do a deal and get the one he wants."

His time at QPR would be an opportunity for Dowie to prove doubters wrong and put a new shine back onto his CV. It was also a chance for him to display some 'bouncebackability' – a word he'd coined back in 2004, when discussing Crystal Palace's up-and-down start to the Premiership season. (The word had gained cult popularity on Sky Sport's Soccer AM. The following year it was even included in the *Collins English Dictionary*, crediting Dowie as its originator.)

When the appointment of Dowie as QPR's first team coach was announced, former boss Gerry Francis, who had Dowie as his assistant manager at the club, said he would be under pressure to produce immediate results. Francis told *The Mirror*: "He will be expected to be up there challenging for promotion with the backing he has got so it will be a big year for him, but he has the experience and the backing behind him to put his plans in place."

When Dowie and Paladini went to see an Italian under-21 tournament at the end of May 2008, they found young players Samuel Di Carmine, Matteo Alberti and Emmanuel Ledesma, who they brought in on loan. Ledesma, in particular, looked a shrewd piece of business as the season began.

While the pressure was undoubtedly being heaped on Dowie, Paladini had to deliver for the new bosses as well. He saw himself as a middleman, ensuring the club moved smoothly. "On the football side of the club, I'm the liaison between Dowie and Flavio, they both come to me with their questions. Flavio, Bernie and Mittal phone all the time to see how we're doing, and on matchdays they always call after the final whistle. But my only contact in the running of the club is with Flavio.

"He makes all the decisions, while Bernie and Mittal want to know what's going on. You won't believe that an hour before a big Grand Prix race, when Flavio's team is working on the car getting everything ready, he's on the phone to me to find out what's going on and how we've played. And he wants to know about every free kick, every chance, everything.

"The interest of the board members has grown over the time they've been here. They won't leave now because the potential is so great. The plan for this season is to aim for the play-offs, minimum. Anything less than that would be very disappointing. But if we are in a position that we are one or two points from the play-offs or promotion and we need to spend three or four million to buy good players to make us stronger, then that's possible. We will do the best we can to get promoted."

The financial constraints that held Paladini back in the past were gone. "I used to have just two players on four grand a week – Lee Cook and Danny Shittu. Other than that it was two and a half thousand a week for the players. Today, we're talking £10,000 a week and that's the deal. That's the reality for QPR if we want to be successful. That's what comes with expectation. When it comes to wages, if you spend up to £4,000 a week, you can only hope not to get relegated.

"If you spend between £5,000 and £8,000, you can guarantee pretty much that you will stay in this division. If you spend between £8,000 and £12,000, then you can aim to get players who can take you into the Premiership. I mean, if you can get £10- or £12,000 playing for Wolves or whoever, why would you come to us and get less? You wouldn't, so you have to pay the rate expected.

"The big sponsors we've got now [Gulf Air and Lotto] are all down to Flavio and Bernie. If they weren't here, there wouldn't be these sponsors at QPR. Before them, sponsorship deals at this club were for £30,000 or £40,000, nothing like the multimillion-pound deals we are talking about now. We've got better sponsorship deals than some clubs in the Premiership."

Paladini insisted the financial developments off the pitch didn't equate with a move to a new stadium; the club's long tradition of playing in the heart of Shepherds Bush was not under threat.

Since the club was formed in 1886, Rangers had laid its collective hat at more grounds than any other club – 12 in total, its west/northwest London locations including Kensal Rise Green, Wormwood Scrubs and Kilburn Cricket Ground.

In 1917, during World War One, the club had taken over a ground at Loftus Road previously occupied by one of London's leading amateur sides, Shepherds Bush FC, which disbanded during the war. Three sides of the ground were unterraced banks at the time, but Loftus Road would evolve into an intimate, atmospheric stadium where fans in the stands felt very close to the pitch, so near that they could almost touch the players. This boxed-in theatre would live on.

As Paladini stressed, "There should be no worries on that front. It will always be QPR, Loftus Road. That's the way we package it to sponsors and corporate clients – QPR, Loftus Road, London. If we get into the Premiership, we could increase the capacity from 18,000 to 28,000 at Loftus Road quite easily and that would be enough for us at this stage. Even if it was 25,000 or 26,000 that would also be OK, because the atmosphere here is good and we don't want to lose that bond with the fans. Everyone at the club knows that."

Vice-chairman Amit Bhatia reiterated that the board had no intention to move and was more likely to expand the stadium. As he explained, "I've often been asked would we keep the stadium at Loftus Road as it is. My answer is that we don't need anything else at the moment. Our stadium is more than adequate. We've spent money on parts of the stadium, which we thought was essential, and some fans wanted to know why.

"We explained that we wanted to attract some big name sponsors, which would help the club in going forward in the future. But when it comes to Loftus Road, if it got to the point that 30,000 crowds were queuing up for every home game, then we would have to extend the stadium, but right now, we're not in that position. If we required it in future, we would consider asking the council about increasing the capacity."

If QPR did get promotion then there was a war chest to fund an assault on the Premiership, offering decent money for the right player. "You've got to remember that in January last season," said Paladini, "these people spent £6m, not including the wages bill, which was unheard of before at this club. I don't wait for the agents to contact me about a player. I've been in this game too long. We go to see the player first. We see the player two or three times.

"Before the takeover, it was very different. I'd look at whether I could afford the wages, or if they were on a free or at the end of their contract, or some other way of making the sums work for us. Now it's changed, the organisation is better. I've got people scouting who know what they're doing. We're looking at tournaments where we can find young players like we did with Ledesma. There's no guarantee that these young players ever deliver like you hope, but I think we did well with Ledesma. Sometimes you can spend £10m and they're rubbish. I believe the future of the club is very good. We are a very professional set-up here."

As the new season kicked off, press speculation was rife that Dowie's job was solely to get QPR out of the Championship and into the Premiership, at which point a bigger name in football management would be drafted in to replace him and lead the club toward bigger goals. But Dowie ignored such talk in the media. He was displaying that famous bouncebackability, with a job many managers in the Championship – even the Premiership itself – would have given their sheepskin coats for. This was the greatest opportunity of his career.

It was sure to be a season where he came under intense pressure and media scrutiny, and, if he didn't come up with the required results, Flavio Briatore would doubtless be breathing down his neck. But it was also a chance to take Rangers on a journey to the promised land of the Premiership.

QPR 2 – 1 Barnsley

9 August, 2008

QPR scorers: Hall (2)

Attendance: 14,964

CHAPTER FOUR

WHEN THE ATMOSPHERE was rocking in Q Block, the seating area in the corner of the stadium between the Loft and Ellerslie Road, it was usually Pete Davies and his drum at the heart of it. The drum was actually given to him by Gianni Paladini, a relic from the days when Wasps rugby team shared the stadium at Loftus Road. And it was Davies behind a number of the QPR fans' favourite chants too.

He remembers how he came up with 'We Are the Rangers Boys', the call to arms that echoed around Loftus Road. "We were on the way to play Southend away, when we got hammered 5-0 [February 2007]. We were sitting on the train going up there, coming up with some ideas for songs. And I said, 'We are the Rangers boys, stand up and make some noise . . .' Well immediately, I thought, that works.

"That night we got thrashed, but I remember – and this is where being slightly obsessive is useful – being at the back of the stand and cracking my hand against this wall in beat with the chant to make some noise, because I just knew this would take off eventually. The front of my hand was all cut – well, you don't worry about it at the time. But the chant really took off a few weeks and a few games later.

"It got to the point at the end of that season where Marcus Bignot and Martin Rowlands were singing 'We Are the Rangers Boys' on the pitch in front of us after the last game of the season. Even the players were singing it. It's a simple chant, easy to get, and for me it's quite uplifting inasmuch as there's only about 10 words but it says quite a lot: 'We are the Rangers boys, stand up and make some noise,' there's a message in that which you hope is inspiring the team. Then over the summer, I learnt they'd turned the chant into a slogan on a t-shirt in the club shop, which means there's blokes walking around Tesco's wearing my chant, which is quite strange when you think about it."

As the new season began with Dowie at the helm, one player seemed to be grabbing the limelight at Loftus Road. It wasn't long before Emmanuel Ledesma would have his own t-shirt in the club shop, emblazoned with his own chant, crafted by Pete Davies and his mates and set to the tune of 'La Bamba'. "We were thinking about what to do with Ledesma. My mate came up to me and said try 'La La La La Ledesma'. He'd heard something similar at Liverpool being sung about Rafa Benitez.

"We thought 'La La La La Ledesma from Argentina . . .' and we sang it in the Springbok pub before the first game of the season against Barnsley, just to see how it would go down. Would the fans pick up on it? Then we added his first name to the song and it became, 'Emmanuel Ledesma from Argentina . . . La La La Ledesma,' slightly different to the song we tried in the Springbok the week before, but it's trial and error with a chant like this until you get it right. It's so difficult to put your finger on it, but you just know when you've got a song that's going to kick off, it's a gut feeling. And I knew that the Ledesma song would take off.

"It was when we played Carlisle United in the Carling Cup, a month later, that it caught on. We saw Ledesma after the second game of the season, at home against Doncaster. We told him about this song we had made up for him, the words and everything, and he said, 'Oh yes . . . very good song.' We asked, 'Did you hear it being sung during the match?' and he said no, he hadn't heard it.

"But the funniest thing was after the Carlisle game, which was a couple of days later, by which time it had really taken off and everyone in Q Block was singing it. He signed a couple of tops for the fans and I said, 'Did you hear it?' and he replied, with a big smile, 'Yes, I heard it.' So the chants can make a difference and inspire the players, I think. By the same token I think booing can affect players as well, and I never boo a QPR player. Never have, never will. The majority of players have got songs written about them, but not all of them take off. It depends on what the fans latch onto and how popular the player is at the time."

Rangers ended up beating Carlisle United 4-0 in the Carling Cup First Round tie and Ledesma got a hat-trick in 29 minutes. After the match all the talk was about the Argentine, who was interviewed by the official club website. He said through an interpreter: "I am very happy at the moment. It's the first hat-trick of my career and I'm delighted to have done it so quickly here at QPR. I am really happy the fans have a song for me already. I hope they will continue to push me on and support the team."

Tim Flowers, assistant coach, said, "He's a good young player, from Argentina via Italy. But he's a kid, a young man still learning his trade and he will be for a long time to come. But he's a lovely lad to have around the place, he's always got a smile on his face."

Flowers confirmed that he understood the club did have first option on Ledesma after his one-year loan from Genoa in Italy's Serie A was complete. "He's clearly a very good player, but we've got to be careful not to overcook it. There's going to be periods when he'll have to come out of the team and have a rest. At the moment, he's on fire, but I'm sure there were scouts seeing that and thinking they can't leave him so much room, but that could free up room for someone else."

Ledesma revealed he'd already had discussions with Briatore about his future. "I really like it here and would like to stay. I've spoken with Flavio Briatore and told him how happy I am here, so what happens in a year happens."

After the defeat against Sheffield United less than a fortnight earlier, Ledesma had come in for some flak. He knew he had to improve his defensive duties, which was something Dowie had worked on with him in training. But now he had both the management and fans singing his praises, which had obviously made an impact on him.

One other song that took off around this time was a gentle ditty about Dowie, sung to the age-old tune of 'Winter Wonderland': "He's ugly as fuck and he's taking us up, living in a Dowie wonderland . . ." But, for some reason or other, Dowie didn't make any mention of his chant on the QPR website.

But not all QPR fans were lucky enough to attend every game and sample the atmosphere in Q Block. Michal McSperrin-Kossak grew up in Hanwell, west London, as a QPR fan during the era that saw Les Ferdinand upfront and Gerry Francis as manager. He remembers watching QPR beat Coventry 0-1 away to go top of the league during the very first season of the Premiership: "The atmosphere around the club in those days was fantastic. A great family club, which was competing with the big boys!"

But he left leafy west London for the less glamorous climes of Krakow, Poland, at the start of 2008. His mother was Polish and, after escaping the London rat race, McSperrin-Kossak decided to work for a company that produced English travel and city guides to over 22 cities across Central and Eastern Europe.

As he explains, "I'm pretty sure that I'm the only QPR fan living in Krakow and I have to really try hard to keep up with QPR over here. I have to pretty much rely on the internet to keep up to speed on things. I'm often on the website forums and news sites, checking the latest rumours and information surrounding the club. It's really frustrating sometimes as I'm not over there in the thick of things in the Loft, but I'm always wearing my shirt when I'm watching or listening to games online. I usually listen to the games online via the official website."

A couple of bars showed Sky Sports games, but QPR was infrequently shown live on TV so following Rangers games from Krakow was a difficult process. "I often have problems with my internet connection and the commentary gets broken up or stops altogether. It always seems to happen just as QPR are on the defensive and sounding vulnerable, so I'm always worried that when I get the feed back again that we'll have gone a goal down or something."

When QPR played Bristol City away, it was a particularly tense affair at Ashton Gate, where the game finished 1-1 and QPR showed great team spirit to hold onto the draw with 10 men after Ledesma was sent off in the 50th minute. It was just as tense in McSperrin-Kossak's apartment in Krakow, about 980 miles away.

"The game against Bristol City was a nightmare because my internet kept getting disconnected every couple of minutes, so I couldn't keep up with the game at all really. I was running back and forth from my computer to the phone socket (at the opposite end of my apartment), and trying to catch just slight titbits of information and commentary.

"I missed both goals as well as Ledesma's sending-off, so I was completely bemused by the whole thing. The commentator said that it was 0-0, then, between trips to the phone socket and me screaming at the broadband modem in a mixture of broken

Polish and English swear words, he came back to say it was 1-0! Cue joyous cheering and shouts of 'You R's!' followed by banging on the floor from my neighbours upstairs.

"Then it happened again! Connection died and Adebola scored. What did I miss? How did it happen? I don't know. But after missing Ledesma's red card, what I did know was that someone at the internet company was going to be getting an earful of angry 'Ponglish' as soon as the final whistle had been blown. I don't think that my neighbours had ever quite heard such a barrage of foul language from someone who was not actually talking to another person."

Living in Poland, he was able to fully appreciate the global appeal of English football; he also saw the obvious potential for QPR if they broke into the higher echelons. "Premiership football as a whole is a global brand without a doubt. Here in Poland you can watch matches live on Polish TV. They are really popular here.

"The Polish league is not very good in quality, so Poles like to watch the Premiership to see all the top players and some great matches. You can buy the shirts of teams like Man United and Chelsea and with so many Poles having been to the UK, they all know the teams and players as well. To survive and be successful, I think we do need to be aiming to become a global brand.

"The fact that Briatore, Mittal and Ecclestone know big names across the world and can use those contacts to help the club is fantastic. There is no way that we would have got someone like Parejo to QPR had Briatore not known Ramon Calderon, Real Madrid's president, that's for sure. These guys have contact lists that make up the rich list of the world and they can really start to call in some favours, which I'm sure they already have done.

"They seem to be trusted by the people that know them, so that can only be good for QPR. If you look at how popular Formula 1 is in Asia and the Far East, it gives us a great opportunity to use that too. If we are associated with that success then people will be interested in us.

"Business these days seems to me to be more about who you know, not what you know, and if that is really true then Rangers are set-up pretty well to make the most of that. But the question is, do we want to be like Man United or Chelsea, or would we like to continue our traditions of being a local, family and community club? It'd be great if we could achieve the success without losing that identity, but I think it is inevitable that we will lose it because football is no longer a sport but a business, and business relies on money. The club will have to change to be competitive."

The new board was fully aware of this potential and set their sights further afield. Through their association with sponsors Gulf Air, the club launched a Football in the Community Programme in Bahrain, the Middle Eastern country where the airline was based. But there was an even bigger market just across the Arabian Sea.

"My father-in-law is very well known in India," Amit Bhatia says of Lakshmi Mittal, the fourth richest man in the world. "There was a time when you would only see shirts from clubs like Real Madrid being worn there but I was in an airport on a recent trip and I saw two young kids wearing QPR shirts and one had Dexter Blackstock's name on the back, which I told him about straight away when I got back. When I was growing up, I never saw this in India.

"Because of our involvement, we get letters to organise local summer camps and youth academies, but we have to find the best way to get involved in the development of football in the Indian market. We would like to develop something sustainable and make it ours. The potential is huge."

As QPR was developing a cult following in India because of the involvement of the Mittals, Bhatia's good friend, the captain of the Indian national side, suggested players he should consider from his homeland. It's impossible to overestimate the potential market for football in India, already the second most populated country on earth with 1.1 billion people, not far behind China's 1.3 billion.

But while the Chinese government's policy of one-child-per-family is expected to maintain the size of their population over the coming decades, India's population is expected to keep on rising. The United Nations reckon it will reach around 1.6 billion by 2050, by which point it will be confirmed as the biggest population in the world as its people attain a higher life expectancy.

When German international goalkeeper Oliver Kahn decided to choose India as the destination for his final match, it generated the most headlines yet about this growing football market. He made his last professional appearance for Bayern Munich in May 2008, at a Calcutta friendly against local champions Mohun Bagan during the German club's Asian tour. Around 120,000 passionate Indian football fans squeezed into the Salt Lake Stadium for the game, which Bayern Munich won 0-3.

A football revolution is quietly taking place, now that football has become the nation's second favourite sport after cricket. It's widely believed that the game could explode in the region if football's equivalent to Indian cricketing legend Sachin Tendulkar is discovered, a player who can make his mark on the international stage.

The new Indian middle classes regularly tune into English Premiership football, with matches screened in bars across Mumbai, Bangalore and other cities, and every game of the I-League – a fledgling professional Indian football league – is also covered on national television, offering a structure to the sport. FIFA, international football's governing body, is fully aware of the potential for expansion that exists in the world's largest democracy.

As Bhatia confirms, "The Oliver Kahn match was a very important game for India. I was recently asked to make a speech at a FIFA-organised event to discuss the potential of developing football in the Indian market and Peter Kenyon, Chelsea's chief executive put his hand up to ask me a question; David Dein, who used to be Arsenal's vice-chairman was there too. We believe our club will be central to the development of the game in the region. We will have a major part to play there." If Bhatia is right then 10 years from now QPR's international profile will be very different to today's, with a fanbase stretching far beyond its traditional heartland in west London.

But the more immediate concern in autumn 2008 was promotion to the Premiership. And Iain Dowie's side was about to nudge its way into the play-off positions.

AUGUST

FIRST TEAM COACH IAIN DOWIE

Swindon 2-3 QPR (Carling Cup R1)

12 August, 2008
Attendance: 7,230
Visiting QPR fans: 1,891
Scorers: Balanta, Blackstock, Delaney

Sheffield United 3-0 QPR

16 August, 2008
Attendance: 25,273
Visiting QPR fans: 1,287
Table: 15th with three points

QPR 2-0 Doncaster Rovers

23 August, 2008
Attendance: 15,536
Scorers: Blackstock, Ledesma
Table: 9th with six points

QPR 4-0 Carlisle United (Carling Cup R2)

26 August, 2008
Attendance: 8,021
Scorers: Ledesma (3), Stewart

Bristol City 1-1 QPR

30 August, 2008
Attendance: 17,543
Visiting QPR fans: 1,525
Scorer: Blackstock
Sent off: Ledesma
Table: 9th with seven points

CHAPTER FIVE

THE GAME AGAINST Southampton in September 2008 was QPR's first televised match of the season on Sky Sports. It was also being shown in Michal McSperrin-Kossak's local bar in Krakow, Poland, so he would be able to watch the team playing live for the first time that season.

During the week leading up to the game, there was plenty of media interest in Briatore and his side, now sitting just outside the play-off positions with seven points from four games. In fact there was a lot of interest in mega-rich foreign investors in English football in general, as Manchester City's new owners, the Abu Dhabi United Group, unveiled a stunning £200m takeover of the Premiership club and proceeded to smash the British transfer fee record, after agreeing £32.5m with Real Madrid for the Brazilian Robinho. They had now replaced QPR as officially the richest club in the world.

As McSperrin-Kossak says, "It's crazy how much money is going into football right now. We have a huge financial crisis looming and yet we still have these billionaires coming along and buying clubs like they are small change in their pocket. I'm actually pleased that we are no longer the world's richest club as it takes us slightly out of the spotlight so that we can get on with building a strong team and club without the constant pressure of that label over our head.

"I do think that QPR is in a different position to the other clubs that are being bought out though. I do believe that the board are building a club and business that will support itself and therefore be much more stable and sustainable going forward than other teams like Manchester City, who reckon they can just buy their way to success and just throw money at it to achieve it."

Briatore made it clear to BBC Radio London before the Southampton game that he and no one else would decide where the club spent its money. "I don't trust anyone with my money. Sometimes I will ask the manager of the bank but not the coach. This is our money, which we want to spend in our direction.

"We will use the knowledge of the coach but I believe everybody needs to do their own job. I want everyone to take the responsibility for one sector. I don't want a one-man band. We have a vision. We want to motivate people for the project. It is not only a question of money but it's a question of complicity between management and players."

He also told Skysports.com that he would not be copying Manchester City's free-spending approach. "In the short time myself and my partners have been involved in English football, we have realised that we must be very careful about our financial responsibilities. We are following a sensible business model because the Championship is a dangerous league in which it is very easy to see large amounts of money leave the club unless it is invested wisely.

"There is no wage cap which means that clubs may gamble and lose – we don't intend to do that. It's not what we want. QPR has spent less money than anyone, and we haven't paid a fee for a player since January; indeed we realised a positive balance of £400,000 for transfer dealings over the summer.

"It puzzles me that people are talking about QPR as a club

spending lots of money as that's not the case. We are still in the process of attracting investors, not exclusively because of their financial power, but because we want them, as people, to be part of our programme."

QPR faced Southampton on Sunday 14 September 2008, the day after Manchester City played hosts to Chelsea – now the two richest clubs in the Premiership. When QPR eased to a 4-1 win over the Saints, who were reduced to 10 men after half an hour, Rangers moved to fourth in the table and a step nearer joining them at top-flight level.

But throughout the match Dowie was constantly standing on the touchline, encouraging and cajoling his players into better performances. They didn't exactly look like Premiership material on this evidence.

Yet they had the perfect start. Dexter Blackstock scored against his former club after only 37 seconds, when the visitors failed to clear a long throw. It got worse for Southampton when Oliver Lancashire was sent off after 30 minutes of his debut for a reckless, two-footed challenge on Damien Delaney.

But if QPR fans thought the game was effectively over and three points were in the bag, they were wrong. Southampton keeper Kelvin Davis blocked the efforts of Blackstock and Delaney until, seven minutes after the break, the 10 men equalised through Adam Lallana.

Dowie had to win this match to ensure a top-six position, and with an hour on the clock he made a double substitution that changed the game, sending on Martin Rowlands and Patrick Agyemang. Just two minutes later Rowlands bent a free-kick for Damion Stewart to score, even though he looked suspiciously offside when the ball was struck. Blackstock netted his second after another 15 minutes and Agyemang scored a fourth in the dying seconds, against tiring defenders.

Post-match, Dowie said his players looked good when attacking, but out of possession they were poor. Michal McSperrin-Kossak, watching from a Krakow bar, wasn't overly impressed either. "I thought the performance was OK, but far from good enough, despite the scoreline.

"It was worrying how easily Southampton managed to break at us on the counter, and that they scored to make it 1-1. As soon as they went down to 10 men, they got better and we got worse. Luckily, we were able to make the advantage of an extra man count, but there is definitely a lot of room for improvement."

Fans wanted to see a step up. They wanted a performance on the pitch that proved the team was progressing towards an automatic promotion place. 10 days later QPR would face their biggest challenge so far, enabling the fans to see exactly how well they compared against a Premiership outfit in a competitive match.

In the Carling Cup Third Round, Rangers drew Aston Villa away – a far sterner test than a 10-man Southampton side that relied on youth with nine players aged 22 and under in their starting line-up. Martin O'Neill's exciting Aston Villa side, in contrast, was made up of hugely-talented English players like Ashley Young, Gabriel Agbonlahor and Gareth Barry, plus the intimidating presence of Norwegian striker John Carew, who had been terrifying Premiership defences all season.

Aston Villa was emerging as a team to challenge the 'Big Four' of Manchester United, Liverpool, Chelsea and Arsenal. At Villa Park fourth in the Championship would face fourth in the Premiership, a landmark game in Dowie's reign so far. He'd been in control at Coventry 12 months earlier, when his side famously dumped Manchester United out of the Carling Cup at Old Trafford at the same stage of the tournament. Could history repeat itself?

In the 58th minute of the game, the Villa keeper, Brad Guza, on his club debut, punched a corner clear which found Daniel Parejo.

He crossed from the right and Damion Stewart rose in a congested six-yard box to powerfully head home the winner in a 0-1 victory.

Peter Lansley, Midlands football correspondent for *The Times*, reported on the match and noted how there did not appear to be a whole division between the two teams currently placed fourth in their respective leagues: "QPR enter the last 16 of the tournament with some talented players liable to flourish on the higher stage. Daniel Parejo and Emmanuel Ledesma were particularly deft. Dowie believes that Akos Buzsaky is capable of top-grade football. More than anything, the back four produced immense performances to repel John Carew."

As a neutral observer, it was interesting to hear his views on the progress Rangers had made so far and how they compared to a top-six Premiership side. He commented: "I only had a snapshot of how QPR are performing this season, but I really liked two things about them.

"Firstly, they kept the ball well. Parejo, this wonderkid from Real Madrid, and Ledesma, from Genoa, both displayed Premiership quality in the way they controlled the ball and possession. Buzsaky also looked good, I know that Dowie seems to rate him very highly. They could keep the ball and take a player on without breaking out in a blind panic, and they could pass the ball around in triangles in the middle of the park.

"Secondly, I liked the way they defended. The back four's power in retrieving the ball was fantastic – there were some big tackles going in. They were clearly playing to a gameplan, where they would quickly regain their shape whenever they lost the ball. And there was a real team spirit out there on the night, so Dowie deserves credit for that."

Dowie was in an upbeat mood during the press conference afterwards. He told the journalists present: "We're not giving too many goals away, we're much more resolute. We got beat heavily at Sheffield United early in the season and I take the blame for that. I got the system wrong. But since then we've become a team with resolve. I've said before how I like the smell of the dressing-room. I'm not talking about liniment, I'm talking about character."

A week before this celebrated victory, Dowie had used exactly the same phrase after watching his 10-man Rangers side beat Norwich away. He obviously saw his team's growing bond as an essential ingredient.

As Peter Lansley observed, "I didn't know what to expect before I saw them, but I was surprised. QPR's best players didn't look out of place alongside Ashley Young and Gareth Barry. The question is can they play like that every week? I think Birmingham City, Wolves and Reading are the best sides in the division but I think Rangers can certainly make the play-offs. But the bottom line is they have to show consistency. Just look at how they played against Derby three days later . . ."

After the final whistle at Villa Park, QPR looked like a club that was going places – a serious candidate for promotion. With a victory over respected Premiership opposition under their belts, Dowie's side seemed tight-knit, confident and destined for a successful Championship campaign.

But that was all about to change suddenly, as Dowie put his job and the club's push for promotion in jeopardy.

SEPTEMBER

FIRST TEAM COACH IAIN DOWIE

QPR 4-1 SOUTHAMPTON
14th September, 2008
Attendance: 13,770
Scorers: Blackstock (2), Stewart, Agyemang
Table: 4th with 10 points

NORWICH 0-1 QPR

17th September, 2008
Attendance: 24,249
Visiting QPR fans: 802
Scorer: Rowlands
Sent off: Connolly
Table: 4th with 13 points

Coventry 1-0 QPR

20th September, 2008
Attendance: 16,718
Visiting QPR fans: 1,782
Table: 4th with 13 points

Aston Villa 0-1 QPR (Carling Cup R3)

24th September, 2008
Attendance: 21,541
Visiting QPR fans: 2,967
Scorer: Stewart

CHAPTER SIX

THROUGHOUT A FOOTBALL season there are pivotal moments that can be looked back on with hindsight as having had huge importance. When QPR played Derby at home in September 2008, this was one such match. Going into the game, fans should have been buoyant; they were fourth in the table and had achieved a headline-grabbing victory over Premiership high-flyers Aston Villa, in the third round of the Carling Cup. But on the morning of the match a story was breaking that seemed almost surreal.

A statement on the club's official website read: "Following a report in one of today's national newspapers, titled 'QPC is definitely a move too far Flavio', QPR Holdings Ltd chairman Flavio Briatore has issued the following statement: 'This is pure fabrication and I don't know where the story has come from. I haven't spoken to anybody about this subject. I don't know the journalist, but I know the story is totally untrue and we will be contacting our lawyers to pursue this matter further. I can categorically deny that there is any truth in this article.'"

Briatore was outraged by speculation in the *Daily Mail* that QPR was considering changing the name of the club to Queens Park City, to emphasise its location in the capital. Of course, this would have been a PR disaster for the new owners; loyal fans were prepared to accept some changes to the club, but never its name – which dated back to its formation in 1886.

In fact the new owners had already made alterations. Over the summer months the hospitality area was completely revamped, with catering now provided by the renowned Cipriani restaurateurs whose bars and restaurants were frequented by the rich and famous around the world – the most well-known being Harry's Bar in Venice, which opened in 1931. Briatore was a partner in Cipriani, opening its branch in Mayfair in 2004, before his latest venture in W12.

Briatore explained he wanted to turn QPR into a 'boutique' football club, which raised more than a few eyebrows in the pubs around Shepherds Bush at the time. As commercial guests visited Loftus Road that season, they were greeted with the word 'Boutique' boldly inscribed across the front foyer – the centrepiece of a sleek, new-look hospitality area that the club said rivalled anything in the Premiership.

The chairman's idea for the club worked in a similar way to a boutique hotel, which might have 50 rooms rather than the 400 rooms of a grand hotel, but would offer a more uniquely personalised experience. This would be the appeal of Loftus Road over bigger venues like Stamford Bridge or the Emirates Stadium.

There was no doubt that the hospitality package for commercial clients had greatly improved and would impress future investors in the club, a business model that could achieve long-term financial rewards if significant money came into QPR. But the boutique experience had little impact, if any, on regulars at the Springbok pub in South Africa Road. For these fans it was seen as an expensive extravagance, existing in a parallel world to their own. They wanted to see money spent on the pitch, not off of it.

Before the last game of the 2007-08 season, against West

Brom, the club also unveiled a new crest, which, while not universally popular, had been accepted without a huge fuss. "I am delighted with the design of the new crest," Briatore said at the time, "which maintains the Queens Park Rangers tradition of blue and white hoops.

"I know how important it is to the fans that the hoops remain, and that was always going to be the case. This is a period of huge transformation at QPR. This new crest is stylish, thrilling and authentic and signifies the start of what we hope will become the most successful period in the club's history."

While Briatore gushed enthusiastically about the new crest, his strenuous denial that a change to the name was even being considered meant fans could dismiss that story as mischief-making in the media. But there was another issue of growing concern which had similar PR implications.

It blew up just at the point when the club was making genuine progress on the pitch. Stories had emerged that QPR was going to hike ticket prices for home matches described as 'category A' games. These were high-profile fixtures where demand for tickets would obviously be at its highest.

Before the introduction of this new system, matchday prices ranged from £20 for the cheapest seats to £35 for the most expensive parts of the stadium. The controversial new structure had three-tiers: it gave category A, B and C matches different prices, depending on various deciding factors. It was also deemed that the Derby match fell into the most expensive category, as revealed on the club's official website on 18 September 2008:

> "Our ultimate goal at Queens Park Rangers Football Club is to reach the Promised Land of the Premiership and to compete with some of the biggest clubs in the country, and in time, across Europe. As such, we are totally committed to

building a sound financial base for the future, upon which we can continue to build for what we all believe will be the most successful period in our club's history.

"As part of this financial restructuring, we need to increase our matchday revenues and as a result, we have introduced a new three-tiered category banding structure, whereby adult matchday prices are determined by the opposition, their league position, and the day of the fixture.

"Matchday prices will vary depending on the part of the ground in which you choose to sit, namely the Platinum, Gold, Silver and Bronze areas. Our forthcoming home fixture against Derby County on Saturday 27th September will be a category A match, where tickets are priced £50 Platinum, £40 Gold, £30 Silver and £20 Bronze respectively.

"Our fixture against Blackpool on Tuesday 30th September will be a category C fixture. Platinum priced seats will be available for £35, while Gold, Silver and Bronze priced seats are £30, £25 and £20 respectively."

Fan groups reacted angrily to the prospect of £50 tickets on sale in the most exclusive parts of the ground – on either side of the directors' box – while tickets in areas like the popular Upper Loft behind the goal rose from £30 to £40. There was feverish talk of protests before and during the Derby game, when the category-A price rises would be introduced. But it was not just the ire of the home fans that attracted media attention. A lot of interest also surrounded the ticket hike for Derby fans and their stern opposition to it.

Derby turned to the Football League to rule on their row with the club. They said that QPR wanted to charge visiting Rams supporters up to £40 to attend the game – £10 more than originally agreed – but Derby had objected and said the price hike was unfair.

(Clubs set their ticket prices before the start of the season and have to submit them to the league. If a club varies the pricing of tickets, then both participating clubs have to agree to any changes.)

Derby's head of communications, Matt McCann, said on a Derby fans' website: "We have stuck by our guns. We have been very firm on this from day one, we don't think it is fair to increase those prices. Hopefully, the Football League will rule on our side. We have just got to hope commonsense prevails."

John Hemsworth, chairman of the Derby County Supporters Club's executive committee, said: "Some fans cannot afford such price increases in the current economic climate. Going to QPR could cost a fan almost £100 if you take into account £40 for a ticket, £20 or more for travel and something to eat and drink.

"My main worry over all this is that if QPR get away with it, other clubs might try to do the same. The prices are going up for QPR supporters as well and apparently they are not happy because they are being stung also."

The home fans were indeed unhappy. The Football League ruled in Derby's favour, which only prevented the price rise for away fans; the maximum price they would have to pay would be £30.

QPR officials then withdrew price increases at the Loft end for home fans, reflecting the prices that would now be on offer to the visiting supporters – £30 for Upper Loft, £25 for Lower Loft – though rises in other parts of the ground stood for the time being. Indeed, the controversial £50 platinum tickets near the directors' box had sold out during the week before the game.

But this hadn't been the first big price rise at Loftus Road during recent months. Prices had already gone up during the summer for season ticket holders, which wasn't exactly a popular move either. A £399 season ticket in the Upper Loft – labelled a 'gold seating area', one of the most popular parts of the ground for long-standing fans – rose to £599, a leap of 50 per cent. The other season ticket prices for 2008-09 were £450 for the bronze seating area, £525 for the silver area and £699 for the most expensive platinum area.

In July 2008, the club had capped the number of season tickets for the first time to 10,000. Deputy managing director Ali Russell said at the time, "The demand for season tickets has been amazing," describing how the club had been inundated with season-ticket renewals and new requests, and had therefore had to cap the number of season tickets to ensure that plenty of matchday tickets were available for fans who either couldn't afford them or couldn't make it to Loftus Road every Saturday.

In the week before the season's opening game against Barnsley, QPR's official website had announced that season tickets were sold out: "Phenomenal demand for season tickets during the summer has seen thousands of fans secure their seats for the R's quest to return to the Premiership, in the first full season since Flavio Briatore, Bernie Ecclestone and the Mittal family completed their takeover of the club."

The decision to put prices up for matchday tickets as well, during only the second month of the season, alienated those QPR fans who traditionally came from working-class areas of west London and would struggle to meet the increased cost. Ticket prices in general were becoming a bone of contention.

On the day of the Derby match, leaflets were distributed by the campaigning group One QPR, under the heading 'Great football, shame about the prices': "We are delighted by the football of the Super Hoops so far this season. The victory over Villa on Wednesday night was our best performance for years. We welcome the investment into the club, which has brought us exciting football and the hope of a return to the top tier of English football. However, we want all our fanbase to enjoy this success and not be priced out of Loftus Road.

"We want Loftus Road to be full every game and the return of the famous Rangers Roar. Let us make our ground a fortress. But to do this we need to fill the ground with fans, not price out our loyal fanbase. We urge the board to now withdraw all price increases and match banding."

But inside the stadium, the Rangers end was not exactly a scene of seething rebellion. There were some expressions of discontent and chanting against the price rises, but no mass protests. Instead, it was Derby's supporters who were in full battle cry, before a ball had even been kicked. "Forty quid, you're having a laugh!" they chanted, followed by a loud chorus of "Greedy bastards!" These chants continued throughout the match.

Perhaps one reason for the slightly odd atmosphere inside the Rangers end was that the draw for the fourth round of the Carling Cup had taken place just before kick-off. QPR had been pitched against Manchester United at Old Trafford, which had captured the fans' imagination straight away. This was a reason to celebrate, while at the same time no one wanted to be priced out of seeing their team. It was an uneasy mix of emotions.

But if the fans felt uncomfortable before kick-off, they felt positively sick by the final whistle. Rangers did not play well, losing 0-2. They had been unbeaten at home until this match but gave up that record without much of a fight, conceding both goals from corner kicks.

Apart from two moments in the second half, when Emmanuel Ledesma's low shot was deflected onto a post by a defender before Dexter Blackstock hit the same upright soon after, it always looked like a game QPR was going to lose. After losing the moral high ground to Derby over ticket prices before kick-off, QPR had lost the battle on the pitch as well. Derby, hovering just above the relegation zone in the Championship, seemed by far the more determined side.

As the final whistle approached, Derby chants of "Greedy

bastards!" were applauded by some disgruntled Rangers fans in the Ellerslie Road stand. After achieving such a high from the result against Aston Villa less than a week before, there was a distinct change in the atmosphere at Loftus Road.

In the post-match press conference, Derby manager Paul Jewell said, "When people are struggling for cash, it would be nice if people could make football more affordable for the guy in the street." He added, "We can't keep bleeding fans dry. We've got to give them something back, otherwise we'll drive them into pubs and they'll watch on TV. We want the grounds full and the atmosphere is what we all thrive on."

Howard Prosser had been editor of the QPR fanzine *In the Loft* for 18 years, from 1988 to 2006, and was angered by the ticket-price hike: "I think the supporters of this club could fill the stadium every week, as we've proved when we've had special promotions that offer £5 tickets for adults and free for kids.

"We've always filled it on those occasions and we could fill it every week now if the price structure was better. These price rises are just wrong, £50 a ticket is more than some Premiership clubs. The worst thing is that there's so much financial wealth coming into the club, that you'd think they didn't have to demand these ticket prices.

"It's very bad timing. When big investors come in, clubs like ours tend to be despised by others. Man City gets it in the Premiership now. Then, if it feels like the club is charging [home and visiting fans] extortionate amounts of money for tickets, that's how clubs get hated."

Prosser insists Rangers fans don't want their club to be hated by opposing supporters visiting Loftus Road. "We made it clear. We don't want ticket price rises."

It was an issue that had to be dealt with. Opinions like those of One QPR, which distributed the protest leaflets before the Derby game, were clearly making an impression on the board.

Less than a month after the Derby game, on 24 October 2008, Amit Bhatia wrote an open letter to QPR fans in which he tried to bring the simmering tension to an end:

Dear supporters,
In recent days and weeks, I have had the chance to interact and speak with many of you – at home, in and around our stadium and also at our away fixtures.

Many of you have expressed excitement at the current and future prospects of the club. Many of you feel the club is on the right, forward moving track. Many of you have greeted us warmly and welcomed us into the QPR family. Firstly, allow me to thank you for all your support.

In much of the conversations we have had, and encouragement that you have given me, some of you have also expressed unhappiness at the increase in ticket prices for category A matches. It is something that we have listened to intently as a board and as shareholders – we have discussed this issue seriously and considered it deeply.

We live in tough economic times and many of you don't need the added burden of higher ticket prices at select fixtures. Your despair was warranted and justified. So, please be assured that with immediate effect and until the end of the season, we will have no category A or B fixtures and tickets for all home fixtures at Loftus Road will be category C.

We appreciate that when you expressed yourselves, the protests were done silently and peacefully, through letters and conversations. Point made and point taken!

We stand corrected on the ticket price increases.

Come on you R's – onwards and upwards . . .

Yours sincerely,
Amit Bhatia

The letter clearly drew a line under the matter – for this season anyway – and indicated to the fans that Bhatia was prepared to listen to their concerns. As the vice-chairman said, "This season has been a learning process for the board and mistakes have been made along the way. But we've learnt from this, that's for sure. When it came to the rise in ticket prices, I think it was very positive that as a club and as shareholders, we chose to react to this. We genuinely got this price rise wrong.

"I think it's important for the board to be flexible. The fans let us know it was a bad move but they did it in a classy way and I was very pleased with how they let their feelings be known to us. I was at the Birmingham game away and a couple of fans wanted to have a conversation about ticket prices with me.

"They said they understood that more money had to be raised but this rise in ticket prices was proving really difficult. They told us we'd increased them too much. It was understood that this was a mistake and that people were being genuinely hurt. We were pleased as a board to be told all this.

"As a business going forward, I wish we made no mistakes at all, but I don't know if that's ever possible. And we reacted accordingly. When I first got involved with the club, I was trying to figure out what needed to be done behind the scenes. My involvement has become more visible over time. I've got to know some of the fans and attended some of the fans' meetings. I've tried to get more involved."

As soon as the open letter to fans appeared on the official QPR website, rumours were rife that Bhatia and Briatore had fallen out over the admission of a mistake about the hike in prices. Briatore was reportedly unhappy about the announcement, but Bhatia denied that any feud existed between the owners:

"The relationship between Flavio, Bernie and myself is very good. I know things have been said in the press that we don't get on, but the fact that Flavio and Bernie were here was one of the main reasons why we got involved in the first place. I've known them for many years previous to this, so the idea that we're not satisfied with each other just isn't correct.

"I'm much more excited that I'm working alongside shareholders and partners who've had so much success in sport, who know how the business side of sport works. We all have our own expertises, but you have to respect what they've achieved in their careers. Our business works out of mutual respect. When we sit on board meetings, it's not about who's younger of age, or who's got a bigger or smaller shareholding.

"As friends and board members, it's about making the right business decisions. Is there a lively debate? Of course there is. For me, it's very healthy that there are different ideas and opinions being expressed about what should happen at QPR. It's a very positive relationship with a great dynamic, because at the end of it all, we're friends. We've holidayed with Flavio and his wife and my wife's great friends with Bernie's daughters. There's very good communication between us. Each of us is just a phone call away and all this means we run the club the right way.

"Our commitment to this club is over the long term. This is just the beginning of our involvement. In the history of QPR, our time here so far is only a very short period. This club has such a long history and we've only started to become part of it. Our plan is to become a Premiership football side but to achieve this correctly. Build the club from the ground up.

"If we'd come in on Day One and splashed lots of cash to get the club promoted, there's a chance that it might not have worked. There are plenty of examples around the country of cash being splashed but not buying success. There's no guarantee that success will follow.

"For me, it's more important that we build this club properly, embracing it. If it took two, three or four years for us to get promotion, in the long-term history of the club, this would be nothing. It's more important that when we get there, we stay there and be competitive there. When we joined QPR, we were 24th out of 24 teams in the Championship.

"The first aim was to save the club from relegation. The aim this season is to be competitive. In my opinion, I would love us to finish in the play-offs. But if we finished seventh or eighth, it's not terrible. We have to manage success. Have to manage it as doing better than the previous season – but, having said all that, I would love us to make the play-offs."

As soon as it was announced that billionaires had taken over the club the fans' expectations had risen, and managing those expectations was one of the biggest problems the board faced. As Bhatia comments, "The expectation of fans is a pressure and we think that's a really good thing. It reminds us that we have to work very hard to deliver. We know we're being watched and that fans expect success. All of the shareholders are used to dealing with pressure, we don't crack under it. We know big things are expected of this club.

"Over the past 12 months, we have been trying to manage those expectations. It's important for us to tell the fans where we stand. They expect big-money signings, but we're asking for some patience from the fans. They've supported the club through thick and thin, and the support has passed down through families from one generation to another. Hopefully they understand we are trying to do this the correct way. I spent a lot of time with the fans and they understand what we're doing. I hope we are promoted at the end of the season. But I'm realistic. I think it will take a couple of years to build this properly."

As former fanzine editor Howard Prosser explains, "The fans seem to really like the Mittals. They've taken a backseat while

Briatore has been the main voice. We never hear from Lakshmi Mittal, but you can see that his son-in-law Amit Bhatia is very passionate about the place. They've got the money, Mittal is the world's fourth richest man, so do they want to own the club outright or do they want to just be investors? Who knows? Maybe as time goes on we'll find out."

This view was echoed on fans' message boards. Simon Skinner, who writes match reports for *QPRnet.com*, says, "When Briatore and Ecclestone came in, and then Mittal, all QPR fans thought, 'Hey, we've got a chance of doing something here.' And when they put the season ticket prices up before the start of the season, we thought, 'Right, they're going to plough loads of money into this thing.'

"My season ticket went up from £399 to £599, but we thought we're on a charge now. I can see why they're doing it like they are. They're trying to make it a cash-rich business and run it properly – not like how Abramovich has done it at Chelsea, by throwing money at the club like it's going out of fashion.

"But I think they've alienated a lot of fans. The average gate is 14-odd thousand. There are clearly a lot of people who can't afford to go. I think if you talk to fans, they're all glad the new owners came. But they might be hoping that Briatore won't be around for long and that maybe the Mittals will take it over.

"Amit Bhatia seems to be the one with the most feeling for the fans and seems to understand their position a bit more, whereas Briatore says, 'I want to make it a boutique club.' But if you look up in South Africa Road, in the posh seats, all you ever see is a load of grey blankets for people to put over their legs. No one ever seems to be sitting there!

"I think, from a fan's point of view, if he sold the club over to the Mittals tomorrow, no one would shed a tear. Which is a shame, because Briatore's been successful in everything he's done in sport before. While in Formula One I'm sure he is totally ruthless, no one seems to pay too much attention to it. He doesn't have 14,000 people sitting there judging him on it.

"Don't get me wrong, Rangers fans are sensible enough to realise that without him the club would almost certainly have gone into administration and been docked points, and we'd have probably ended up in a similar situation to Luton, who'll get relegated this season. It's all quite a sad state of affairs, to be honest."

Amit Bhatia was emerging as the populist on the board, prepared to talk with and listen to the fans, while Briatore was painted as the flamboyant, tough-talking chairman who does what he thinks right for the business. Fans were picking up these conflicting messages from what they read and saw in the media.

How much of this was true and how much was just newspaper talk remained unknown to anyone outside a QPR boardroom. But Briatore's involvement in football matters – or interference, as his critics might call it – would come under ever-closer scrutiny during the weeks ahead, as the club entered one of its most turbulent periods of the season.

The next game after the Derby defeat was Blackpool at home, a 1-1 draw and another poor performance in the first half, leading to disquiet in the stands. Dowie started the game with Dexter Blackstock as a lone striker, but when Blackpool scored a section of the crowd started chanting, "4-4-2! 4-4-2!" in a bid to force Dowie's hand.

They wanted changes to the player formation and, with Rangers still behind at the break, boos rang around Loftus Road at halftime. But the fans got what they wanted when Patrick Agyemang was introduced as a second striker to support Blackstock in the second half. The game was transformed, with constant pressure from QPR and the inevitable equaliser scored by Blackstock.

But next came an away defeat to Birmingham City. Suddenly, the knives were out for Dowie. QPR had slipped to 11th in the table and – depending on which paper you read – either former manager Terry Venables or Millwall boss Kenny Jackett was being lined up to replace him.

Briatore and Dowie held crisis talks to discuss this run of bad form, but the first team coach survived with his job still intact. As Rangers prepared to play bottom-of-the-table Nottingham Forest at home, Dowie told the press, "This season we have played 13 games and won seven of them and we are also in the last 16 of the Carling Cup. I can't affect what these rumours will do to the players. All I can do is my job, get my head down and work hard.

"Whoever wants to make mischief and start these stories, they can do that. But I'm not going to be involved in negativity – I don't believe in it. I will concentrate on doing what I am doing. This is whispering tittle-tattle, and until it comes to fruition, I'm not going to worry about it. I know I am doing a decent job here and I think I have got the support of the players, which is the most important thing."

But, as a wise man once said, a week is a long time in football. Dowie's fate would be sealed in seven days.

His team was inspired by the return of Akos Buzsaky to midfield after a spell out due to injury to beat Nottingham Forest, without looking too impressive on the pitch. Buzsaky stood out as the difference between the teams; the Hungarian international had missed the opening six weeks of the season due to an ankle operation undergone in the summer. His match fitness was improving and he showed glimpses of what the fans had missed from him so far that season. QPR won 2-1, with Buzsaky scoring the winner.

The bottom line for Dowie was that his team had beaten Nottingham Forest and had three more points on the board. But he remained at the eye of a storm, as rumours swirled around about his job being under threat and he continued to lose his battle to win over the fans.

Simon Skinner from *QPRnet.com* commented, "Dowie was one of the more underwhelming appointments ever made. But when he first came in we could see that he'd noticeably made the team much fitter than they were. Bringing in John Harbin as performance manager was probably the best thing he ever did for the club.

"Last season under De Canio, we'd be two up after 80 minutes then concede two and lose two points. Now it's different, for instance the game at Norwich away from home when Matt Connolly was sent off in the first half [for two yellow cards] and we had to defend with a rearguard action for 60 minutes. QPR wouldn't have been able to do that last season. But the problem under Dowie was that the football wasn't great. And the game that sticks in my mind, and probably the minds of all the Rangers fans who were there, is the 0-0 draw away at Swansea."

This is an edited version of Simon Skinner's report for *QPRnet.com* on the Swansea match:

"Taken at face value and with no knowledge of this game and how it panned out, a goalless draw away at Swansea sounds like a decent result. Anyone that was there will attest to the fact that this was one of the most negative displays of football ever witnessed and the folly was only added to by the fact that Rangers failed to register a single shot in anger against an outfield player playing in goal.

"On twenty seven minutes, the moment the game really turned away from Rangers occurred. Leigertwood slipped a through ball past the Swansea defence and in a rare moment of attacking play, Rowlands surged from midfield in pursuit. Dorus De Vries in the Swansea goal was quickly off his line.

"He slid in and Rowlands slid in and there was an almighty

collision. The physio was quickly on and signalled straight away that De Vries was done for the night. It transpired that he had a fractured cheek and jaw. In my opinion, the ball was there to be won and Rowlands certainly didn't try to do the keeper. He was rightly cautioned.

"It soon became clear to the R's fans that there was no keeper on the Swansea bench as Alan Tate made a hasty change into a keeper's kit on the touchline. The defender was nominated sub keeper as Martinez generally doesn't have one on his bench which I always find odd. It mattered little though as the quite pathetic Rangers passing game failed to force him into a solitary save for the remainder of the game.

"The final whistle brought a huge sigh of relief from the R's fans as well as a burning sense of anger that many had driven the thick end of 400 miles and shelled out God knows how much to watch a team show absolutely no attacking intentions whatsoever.

"Dowie says he wasn't happy with the display but I don't buy that. The team started negatively and got worse, he could have changed it but he didn't, he let it fester. A negative mindset couldn't be shaken off and to fail to have a single shot in anger at a bloody defender in goal is unforgivable.

"As I said at the start, on face value this is a good point. Had Swansea had anyone in the side that could finish a sandwich then they would have smashed Rangers to pieces but they didn't, so they didn't. Chances have to be taken when they arrive and they couldn't do it. They were the only team doing any sort of attacking yet they get the same reward as a team that doesn't want to get out of their own half.

"One thing I do know is that if Rangers had passed a team to death at Loftus Road for a nil-nil then they would have been booed off at the end!"

The 500 travelling fans were irate on the long trip home from

South Wales. It was clear that something had to change. "They had a right-back in goal for more than an hour and we didn't have a shot on target!" Simon said. "I kept shouting at players, just shoot, have a shot at goal, do something . . . anything! It was a horrendous game.

"Fairly or unfairly, Dowie's got a reputation as a long-ball manager, probably because of the sort of player he was – a big, old-fashioned target man. Now that doesn't necessarily mean he'll play like that as a manager, but that became the style he was tagged with.

"The football wasn't as interesting to watch as with De Canio, who had us playing some fantastic football. With Dowie, we were tighter at the back, but more boring going forward. Then there was that Swansea game. Football fans are usually fairly good indicators of how things are with their humour and once, when we shot over the bar during that game, the whole away end erupted. The players on the pitch must have seen that and groaned, 'Fucking hell, they're not happy . . .' Dowie was on a hiding to nothing. He clearly wasn't Briatore's man."

Rangers had won only one of their last five matches and were ninth in the table, which simply was not good enough for Briatore and the board. They had a meeting to discuss Dowie's position and a club statement was released three days after the Swansea game, on Friday 24 October 2008. It read:

"The board of Queens Park Rangers Football Club has terminated the contract of manager Iain Dowie with immediate effect. Dowie, who took over the reins at Loftus Road in the summer, oversaw 15 matches in charge in all competitions and leaves the R's ninth in the Coca Cola Championship."

Dowie was the first Championship manager to lose his job that season. (He had previous experience of 'winning' the sack race after losing his job at Charlton two years before, also 15 games into the season.) He was the second manager to leave the club in six months, following the departure of Luigi De Canio in May.

Gareth Ainsworth, already on the coaching staff, was appointed caretaker manager as stories quickly spread about a possible successor. Former Inter Milan boss Roberto Mancini had been spotted in London during the week and was immediately linked with the vacant post, but his agent dismissed the speculation, stressing that he was in London just to watch the Champions League clash between Chelsea and Roma at Stamford Bridge, and to take English lessons.

QPR midfielder Gavin Mahon admitted he was surprised by Dowie's sacking, which took place after a session at the club's training ground in Harlington, Middlesex, on the Friday morning before playing Reading away. As he told BBC Radio London, "Just after training Flavio Briatore said he wanted a meeting with everyone and said that Iain's leaving. It was strange because the gaffer had been taking training. 20 minutes later we were told by the chairman to go to a meeting and that's where we found out. I was a little bit shocked, but I've had all sorts of things in my career.

"On a personal note, I got on really well with Iain. The coaching was top drawer, well organised, everyone was fit and at times we let him down on the pitch with our performances. His record's decent, you can't fault it. We've got a decent cup game coming up [Manchester United in the Carling Cup fourth round] and are in a decent position in the league. Everyone knows how hard this league is. I think this club has moved on a lot from last year."

The sports pages of the national newspapers focussed on tensions in the relationship between Dowie and Briatore. "I was not happy with the football that Dowie was producing, simple as that," Briatore told *The Times*. "I know what I am doing. I have won World Championships in Formula One. I am from the sport business."

Predictions at the start of the season that QPR would be among the favourites for promotion – thanks to the financial muscle of Briatore, Ecclestone and Mittal – had made Dowie's departure so early into the season a big story. Dowie was reported to have clashed with Briatore over players who came to the club thanks to the chairman's network of sport contacts across Europe.

The foreign footballers who had joined QPR this season included 34-year-old Italian ex-international midfielder Damiano Tommasi, who had 25 caps and more than 250 appearances over an illustrious 10-year spell for Serie A side Roma. He joined the club in September 2008 from the Spanish team Lavante, on a contract until the end of the season, but had yet to make an appearance.

The press also suggested that Briatore was rankled by Dowie's reluctance to grant rising Spanish star Daniel Parejo a regular starting role. Briatore had announced Parejo's arrival, on loan from La Liga giants Real Madrid, just before the start of the season amid great fanfare. The chairman enjoyed his coup and Parejo was tipped as a superstar in waiting, but he found it hard to establish himself in the Championship with QPR.

"I liked Dowie initially," says Howard Prosser. "He'd been at QPR in the 1990's and was an assistant manager to Gerry Francis, so he already had a link with the club, which helped. I thought he was an odd choice when he was chosen by the new board to come back to QPR, but I was prepared to give him a fair crack, and when he was sacked it was still quite a shock.

"There was a moment, when we beat Aston Villa, when his name was being chanted around the stadium. That felt like he'd won over the doubters, and I thought he was doing fine under the circumstances until then. But you wonder how much the team was his selection and how many players were forced upon him.

"On the pitch, he didn't really build on those two victories against Villa and Southampton. I think there were increasingly questions about his policy of playing just one player up front. It wasn't very popular with fans, especially when we weren't winning.

"And there were stories of tension behind the scenes between him and Briatore. I think Dowie had every right to stand his ground if he felt that decisions were being forced on him. I just don't know how much of an idea he had of what he was getting himself into when he took the job, but I think the next man certainly will."

Matters came to a head the day before an away game to Reading, when Dowie was sacked. Speculation in the media and among QPR fans about board interference in team matters was intense.

In his *Times* interview, Briatore dismissed claims that he had tried to influence Dowie's team selection before the Reading match: "It was just a normal discussion. The coach is important, but the money is coming from us. If we had not made the decision about Dowie, the season could have been a big disaster. I'm not scared to make a decision. Not making a decision is often a bad decision. In the papers they say that I choose the team, but this is crazy."

There were two clearly conflicting positions emerging over Dowie's dismissal. The football press talked of tension within the club and interference by the chairman, which the official line coming out of Loftus Road dismissed as totally untrue. Amit Bhatia backed his chairman under fire and insisted Briatore was not getting involved in team selection. "We heard the rumours about interference in picking the team but that is not at all the situation," he insisted.

"Do we care about the team, how players are progressing? The honest truth is of course we do. But any talk of Flavio picking the team is simply not true. A lot of the time that this was being said in the press, the Formula One season was on and he was at a Grand Prix in Brazil or China. We definitely like to feel part of the team and know how the coach is feeling, but any talk of board interference is just paper talk and completely untrue. I can't stress that enough."

SEPTEMBER/OCTOBER

FIRST TEAM COACH IAIN DOWIE

QPR 0-2 Derby
27th September, 2008
Attendance: 14,311
Table: 5th with 13 points

QPR 1-1 Blackpool
30th September, 2008
Attendance: 12,500
Scorer: Blackstock
Table: 8th with 14 points

Birmingham City 1-0 QPR
4th October, 2008
Attendance: 18,498
Visiting QPR fans: 725
Table: 11th with 14 points

QPR 2-1 Nottingham Forest
18th October, 2008
Attendance: 15,122
Scorers: Balanta, Buzsaky
Table: 6th with 17 points

Swansea 0-0 QPR
21st October, 2008
Attendance: 13,475
Visiting QPR fans: 493
Table: 9th with 18 points

CHAPTER SEVEN

THE DISMISSAL OF Iain Dowie was a crucial moment in the reign of the new billionaire owners. Emotions were riding high at Loftus Road after just three months of the new season. The honeymoon period for the new board was clearly over. Message boards were crammed with frustrated opinion. This was supposed to be a season full of promise, but many fans believed the dream of glorious promotion to the Premiership was already turning sour.

The owners clearly wanted to build their long-term project around the first team coach who they believed was the right man for the job. But fans were voicing their concerns in pubs across west London; some felt uneasy or impatient at unfolding events; others were left bemused by how messy the season was becoming. Dissatisfaction was in the air in W12.

To fully understand the fired-up emotions during this period, it's important to grasp the craziness of the past few years which had seen the club teetering on the edge of financial ruin. Below are the stories of two people at the centre of what was happening – both on and off the pitch – during the unpredictable era before the takeover.

THE FAN'S STORY – ROBERT ELMS

Broadcaster and writer Robert Elms was one of the first QPR fans to know that Dowie had been chosen by Briatore to replace De Canio in the summer of 2008. He was writing an article about Briatore for *GQ* at the time, and was told the news before it was officially announced to the public. "I thought Dowie was a strange choice from the start. I suspect Briatore was talked into that, by someone who said you've got to have an English football man.

"I think, as much as anything, it was about the fact that Dowie is a rather dour man, and whatever you think about Briatore and Ecclestone, they're not dour men. And this slightly bluff, rather grumpy, square-jawed guy, giving off those kinds of vibes, was not what they associated with their pretty football team. Dowie clearly has a record of rubbing chairmen up the wrong way. This is not unique to Queens Park Rangers. But I suspected from the moment he was appointed that it would end in tears, and I think quite a lot of people probably did. It was going to end in promotion or tears, there was no other option."

Elms comes from a QPR family with solid roots in west London. His father was from Latimer Road and his mum from East Acton, so Loftus Road was full of his aunts, uncles and cousins when he was growing up. As a writer he made his name on eighties style bible *The Face*. But he became best known to Londoners as a presenter since the 1990's on the BBC's local radio station, currently known as BBC London 94.9.

He'd watched closely the unfolding events around the takeover by Briatore, Ecclestone and Mittal, because he longed for the club's financial problems to be resolved and for the team he'd supported all his life to thrive once more. "For me, QPR means family," Elms explains of the club's vitally important role in his life. "My father was a QPR fan, my son Alfie is too. But also, it means a broader sense of family. When I walk into Loftus Road it feels like I'm going home. It feels like I'm stepping into somewhere I've known all my life. I know lots of other QPR fans and that's what it means to me.

"Not family in any corny marketing sense – no one ever swears and it's a 'family experience' and all that kind of stuff – because families aren't like that. They argue with each other and they shout. But I think our sense of family comes from our geography.

"We're a little club wedged in between others. Everyone who supports Rangers has some sort of connection to that bit of west London. We're in a very condensed area, and it's very unusual to find anyone who doesn't support Rangers for a geographical reason; either you lived in the area around W12 or your dad did, or your uncle or someone else in your family did. It's linked to that particular bit of London and my family on both sides came from that area."

For Elms, his deep emotional bond with QPR stems from the relationship he had with his father. "The first season my dad took me was the 1966-67 season. It was quite sad. I was six at the time but he died that year, aged 41. He never got to see them promoted, never got to see them get to Wembley in the 1967 League Cup Final. He'd supported them all his life but never saw them play above the old third division.

"And partly that's why I've stayed so loyal to Rangers. I've got two older brothers, and we moved from west London to north London soon after that. They became Arsenal fans, because all the local kids were Arsenal, but because my dad died just at that point in my life, just after he took me to my first game, I stayed with Rangers. It was always a big thing for me to keep what he loved alive. And it was very important for me to take my son Alfie to see Rangers too, so that the family tradition would continue."

During more than 40 years of supporting the club Elms witnessed the great eras at Loftus Road, the teams built around the exquisite skills of Rodney Marsh, Stan Bowles, Roy Wegerle and Les Ferdinand, iconic figures for different generations of Rangers fans. But he also watched with horror as financial troubles took an iron grip on QPR in the nineties.

"I've been very lucky," he says. "I've seen Rangers play at the very highest level. I saw pretty much every game of the 1975-76 season, home and away, when we came second in the league, and I saw that great side of Stan Bowles and Gerry Francis in Europe too.

"I've seen Rangers do well. And to be honest, it was only when we started falling, when we got relegated and relegated again, and ended up back in the third division, where we were when my dad first took me, that I saw a need to get involved in the club in any way. Up until then, I'd been a supporter but a fairly passive one. But suddenly it became apparent that this club was in real danger of going under."

Concerns about the future were not new at Loftus Road. There was always a chance that a club the size of QPR could lose its identity in a merger with another football club in west London, that a businessman would consider it better to have a club double the size. Elms explains, "I was on the pitch protesting about the threat of a merger with Fulham in 1987 and creating Fulham Park Rangers. Do you remember when that was proposed? Fans made it clear they would never let that happen.

"But there's always been a sense that this little club might not be able to survive in the big world, if you know what I mean. It brought it home when Fulham went one way and we went the other. A lot of my mates are Fulham fans, and I've always looked on them as a struggling club with no money.

"And when it all happened to us and we went into receivership, and you found out what that really meant, I honestly thought that there may not be a club to support anymore. I was getting worried by the time we were back in the third tier of English football."

The mood around Loftus Road was changing. The 'third tier' was known at the time as Division Two, where QPR spent three seasons. Charismatic Ian Holloway was at the helm and he would have a huge impact on both the club and the fans. But he faced an uphill struggle to get the club back to where the fans believed it truly belonged.

"When Ian Holloway came, we didn't have that many professional players on the books, and it looked really precarious. That happened around about the same time that something else important occurred – the internet started to really kick in with fans' forums.

"You had a chance to communicate in a way that fans had never done before. You would still talk to the guy next to you in the ground and in the bar, but suddenly there was a network of fans, and what that did at Rangers was make people aware of what was happening at the club – perhaps too much. Before we didn't know and perhaps that was better. It was a better place to be. But suddenly I did know that nobody involved in the club really had any money, and I knew that we had really bad debts.

"They had to borrow that money, and when it got to the point that our club was effectively owned by a Panamanian corporation who no one seemed to know anything about, and couldn't afford to pay the taxman, it dawned on you how potentially disastrous it all really was.

"I said to my son Alfie there was a chance that we could watch Rangers from behind a rope, playing on Paddington Rec. I really thought it could come to that. Or, if we survived, there was a chance we could end up like Brentford or Leyton Orient, a perennially lower-division club, playing in front of 8,000 people in an increasingly decrepit stadium. And this nearly took place, except that the fans stopped it from happening."

In 2003-04, the season QPR got promoted from Division Two, the fans believed they'd played their part in moving the club forward. "Ian Holloway got us back to a half-decent side, I think he did tremendously well. There was also an era in Division Two when everyone playing seemed to be a Rangers fan – Kevin Gallen and Marc Bircham, and Lee Cook was there for a while on loan – so there was a real sense that fans were playing on the pitch and of it being a fans' club; well, it felt like there was no one else running it.

"I went onto a website and said, 'There are big rumours that if we don't raise some money, we are going to go under; we're going to have to sell players as we push for promotion. We've got to try to do something about this. I don't have loads of money, but I'm prepared to put in a bit, and if I can find 100 people who can put in £1,000, then we'll be alright."

Elms got a phone call from campaigning fans' group QPR First, who were interested in his proposal to raise much-needed money for the club. Then other fans groups were contacted, including the official supporters' club, and the reaction was very positive. These different groups didn't always see eye to eye in the past, says Elms, but the initiative was crossing the divides between them.

"Basically, it ended up with six people sitting around my kitchen table in my home. And most of them didn't have any money. I was the only one physically with any money to put into the club there and then. But they were representatives of groups like the Loyal Supporters Association and QPR First, and we just said, 'What can we do together?'

"We came up with the name Our QPR, which we thought was a good name, and the club was completely behind me because basically they didn't have any money, and this was one way of potentially paying the electricity bill. So I went onto the pitch the next weekend and made a little speech, saying we all realised this was a pivotal season and we had to raise some money and support this fantastic club.

"I put in a few grand, not huge amounts, and everyone I knew who could put in £150 or £250 did so. Plus, we contacted former footballers. Do you know the only former Rangers player who paid anything into the fund? (And we contacted many.) It was Peter Crouch, who sent a £1000 cheque straight away, which was great."

Our QPR was launched at the end of 2003, with the aim of paying off the club's immediate debts that season. There were many fund-raising initiatives, including a sponsored walk to Brentford, but if one single image perfectly illustrated how bad the financial situation had got, and how low the club had fallen since the glamorous eras of Rodney Marsh, Stan Bowles and Les Ferdinand, it was the sight of bucket collections outside the stadium.

"My son had a bucket and old boys were putting a tenner into it," says Elms. "It's a fairly working-class fanbase at Rangers, and for pensioners to give you 10 or 20 quid was fantastic."

The campaign raised some serious money – about £70,000 in all – and even the manager himself could see the benefits. "Ian Holloway rang me up and said I really want to buy this player and the club can't afford it. It was Jamie Cureton, he was playing in Korea and he hated it.

"The season before he'd got lots of goals for Reading, but then they'd got promoted and let him go. And he ended up playing for the biggest club in South Korea, Busan I.cons, who said they wanted £30,000 to buy out his contract. We also paid his wages until the end of the season, and we did a deal on the money.

"It was £500 a game, plus £500 appearance fee plus £500 a goal – and this was paid until the end of the season. We were two thirds of the way through by then. I did at one point think he would have to come and live in my house because he flew over from Korea and had nowhere to stay.

"I remember saying to my wife, 'Darling, we may have to put up a footballer in our house!' But it wasn't just me. I really don't want to exclude any of the other people who were involved in all the hard work. Everyone did their bit to raise money for the club. It just showed what QPR meant to so many people and it just felt like it was the right thing to do."

When Cureton scored two goals in a 3-2 victory over Port Vale in March 2004, including a winner in the last minute of the match, there was a real and significant benefit from all the hard work. "I remember after that game, it always stuck in the back of my mind that if we didn't buy him and he didn't score those two goals, we may not have gone up, because we only went up by one point that season.

"So there's just a possibility that what we did – and I do mean 'we' collectively, all those fans who helped to raise money in some way – may just have helped Rangers go up. And more importantly, there's a real possibility that if we didn't go up that season that it may never have happened, that we might still be down there now. We certainly wouldn't have been bought by the people we've been bought by now if we were still in that division.

"The other thing I remember at the end of it all, having rattled all those buckets, was that I felt like I'd done my bit. There was nothing more I could do. I couldn't ring the same people up again to appeal for more money. I didn't have any more money to put in myself. And I didn't want to keep doing it because there was a lot of grief that went with it all.

"As much as most people supported you, there was always a small group of people who thought you were doing it for your own self-aggrandisement, or you were part of some plot with your nose in the trough. So by the end of it, while I wasn't unhappy I had done it, I thought, 'I'm not doing that again.' I felt us, as fans, had done what we could do."

QPR were promoted in May 2004. They beat Sheffield Wednesday 1-3 at Hillsborough in an emotional final game of the season to gain entry to the Championship, pipping Bristol City to second spot by just a single point. An incredible season of tension, grit and determination had come to a glorious end.

"The way I personally remember that season is that when we finally went up, gaining promotion during that amazing day at Sheffield Wednesday, it felt like a massive relief. It felt like we had to drag this club over the finishing line. I think quite literally the fans got them promoted that year. But I've also got to say that those last two seasons in Division Two included some of the best games I'd ever watched at Rangers.

"When we beat Oldham in the play-off semi-final at Loftus Road the year before, it was an unbelievable atmosphere, one that hasn't been matched since. Although the football wasn't of the best quality, those games were so intense and so passionate. We were getting 15- or 16,000 crowds on a regular weekly basis, and taking 2- or 3,000 away to places like Peterborough. I think we all remember the atmosphere and the bond between the fans back then very fondly."

That era of financial crisis came to an end when Flavio Briatore and Bernie Ecclestone bought the club. "I thought thank God they were buying the club, to be honest. It's not as if I haven't had some second thoughts about the takeover since then, but at the time it was just a huge sigh of relief, partly because being a Rangers fan in the preceding years had got less and less about football and more and more about boardroom struggles. I just wanted to sit back and watch a football game again. I wanted to remember what that was like. To not have to go to the game and think, 'Have they paid the bills? Are they going to be able to put the floodlights on?' because all of that was just tiring.

"A little bit of me knew straight away that we were

relinquishing our club when they took over. That the sense of ownership of the club that had been there through the very turbulent period of buckets was about to go. I'm not stupid, it was rational. What we had at Queens Park Rangers during that period was special, because we were in this dire and ridiculous state, probably more perilous than any other club.

"Allegations of guns in boardrooms, boardroom coups . . . it was mad, it was so nutty it was almost like living in this strange thriller with a football match attached, and the football almost seemed less important than the other stuff, so I just wanted to get back to watching a football team. I don't think we were a football team for a while, we were a mad melodrama.

"Now that we have these new owners, people are talking about us being successful, but it depends on what you mean by successful. I don't think we'll ever become Arsenal. I certainly don't want us to become Chelsea. There was this big debate on the Rangers message boards when they took over, and almost everyone to a man said we don't want to be Chelsea. We are Rangers, we are different, we are little and we are local. We are all those things. But there was an immediate collective recognition that the very close bonds, probably unhealthily close bonds, we've had with the club over the previous few years were about to be severed.

"But the most important thing about the arrival of Briatore and the new board is that I'm glad my son still has a team to support. I think most of us older and wiser heads realised there was a distinct possibility that there might not be a QPR team to pass on to our children. That's the most important thing for me, because QPR is all about family."

The tradition passed down to Elms by his late father would live on.

THE PLAYER'S STORY – MARC BIRCHAM

Marc Bircham was born in Wembley in 1978, into a family of passionate QPR supporters. He played for Rangers from 2002 to 2007, clocking up 152 appearances and seven goals for the club he'd supported as a child.

He joined as QPR was coming out of administration and left just weeks before Flavio Briatore and Bernie Ecclestone bought the club. So he was present throughout the period when Rangers struggled with financial insecurity, the darkest days of the club's modern history.

"Like probably 80 per cent of all QPR fans, supporting the club was handed down to me," says Bircham. "It's not your choice. Most QPR fans become fans because they live near the ground or because of their family and that's the way it was with me. My granddad was a QPR fan, my dad was and that was passed down to me and my brothers. You're not going to choose to support QPR. We've not had that many great times. But when we do have them, it makes them even sweeter.

"The first generation of fans emerged around the 1967 League Cup Final. They were a little club before that, then all the locals started supporting QPR and they've had a solid fanbase ever since, passing it down from father to son. There aren't many clubs in London who regularly get 14,000 or 15,000, even now.

"When I joined, we'd just come out of administration. The club priced it to get the fans in, and we were nicking fans off other clubs. A dad couldn't afford to take two kids to see Chelsea or Fulham back then, but when I was at QPR it was affordable.

"That's one of the things about the people who've come in to buy the club. Don't get me wrong, they saved the club. I left in the summer and they were seven days away from going bust, going back into administration.

"Then they changed the badge and I liked the old badge, but

they could get away with it because they were saving the club. But it's one thing changing the badge, changing the kit and hoping to win the fans over, but as soon as you start losing matches, all the frustration comes out from the fans and I think that's what's happening."

There were a few clubs interested in Bircham when he was at Millwall. He'd agreed to move to Birmingham City, who were promoted to the Premiership and wanted him as a squad player. "I could have gone to Birmingham. Then QPR came in for me and the only reason I kicked a ball was to play for QPR. If I didn't do it then I may not have had another chance to do it in my entire career.

"People advised me against signing, saying I should play at the highest level I could. But the way I saw it, I could have played 400 Premier League games, but if I didn't play for QPR it would have been a failure. We sat in Ian Holloway's office, overlooking the pitch, and he told me all about his plans for Rangers. It pulled on my heartstrings and I said, 'I really want to join you. Here's my contract from Birmingham. I know you can't match it but try to get as near to it as possible.'

In this era before QPR was bankrolled by Briatore's millions and Mittal's billions, the Winton family were often QPR's financial saviours. Alex and Matt Winton were major contributors to QPR's transfer funds. The brothers – fans who made their fortune running Ghost Menswear – financed the £250,000 signing of defender Danny Shittu from Charlton in January 2002, and agreed to pay the wages and accommodation of French striker Doudou the summer before.

Along with their father Harold and another wealthy supporter, Maurice Fitzgerald, they set up a company with the express aim of raising further money to allow Ian Holloway to bring in new signings and cover the wages of players. In 2004, Harold Winton was made QPR's Honorary Life President to mark the good work he did in bringing quality players to the club.

"In the end the club paid half my wages and the Winton brothers paid half my wages," explains Bircham. "And I've got a lot to thank the Wintons for because I couldn't take that kind of cut in wages. I had one boy and one on the way. But to have a chance to play for QPR was blinding.

"It wasn't until that first time I ran onto the pitch wearing a QPR kit that it really hit home I was playing for Rangers, and just training every day in QPR gear that I would have bought from the shop before was just unbelievable. I would say to any QPR fan, 'How would it feel for you to play for your club?' Well, that's how it felt to me. My only concern was if it didn't go well and the fans started booing me. I didn't want that to affect my love for the club."

Bircham's passion for Rangers meant he was always going to be popular with the fans, because it showed . . . literally. "My brother said, 'If you ever play for QPR you'll have to dye your hair blue and white,' which of course I never thought would happen," he explains.

"But you know how it is, you say yes to something and it comes back to bite you on the arse. I remember pre-season before my first game, we had a night out on the drink and I was having a chat with Kevin Gallen who, of course, grew up as a QPR fan as well, and we were arguing about who's the biggest fan and it turned out to be me," he reveals with a smile.

"I am the first ever official QPR member to have played for the club. I was a Junior R and I was an LSA [Loyal Supporters Association] member as well – I was all three, so I threw that at him. And I bet him £250 I'd dye my hair blue and white for the first game of the season, which I did. I think I got booked in my first three games, so Olly had a word and said, 'Can you change it back because you're drawing too much attention to yourself?'"

But a cult had already been born. Bircham started getting letters and pictures from parents whose kids had dyed their hair blue and white. Some were saying they couldn't get rid of the colouring and their kids were being suspended from school.

"During the season I kept adding a little bit, and that built up to the play-off final when it was everywhere." Bircham's blue and white hair achieved such recognition that he was sponsored by two hair product companies, Schwarzkopf and Fudge. The Hairdresser of the Year would even be flown down from Scotland when he wanted a haircut.

The chant from Q Block summed up Bircham and what he meant to the fans:

"We love you Bircham, / Because you've got blue hair, / We love you Bircham, / Because you're everywhere, / We love you Bircham, / Rangers through and through . . ."

There was financial insecurity off the pitch, but a special bond was building between the players and the fans. The fact that both Bircham and Kevin Gallen were boyhood supporters of the club added to the chemistry, most clearly evident during a couple of landmark games during the 2002-03 season, as Rangers won their way through to the Division Two Play-off Final against Cardiff at the Millennium Stadium.

"One of my greatest memories at QPR was the winning goal I scored in the last minute of our game against Brentford that season. It was a crucial derby game at Griffin Park that we had to win to stay in the play-off places. A corner came over and I volleyed it from the edge of the box.

"Kevin Gallen said it was the most celebrated goal since Clive Allen scored against West Brom in the 1982 FA Cup Semi-Final. It was fantastic to run over to the fans, who were going mental. I was wearing a retro eighties Rangers shirt underneath my top, one with Guinness as the sponsor on the front, and I took my top off for the celebrations."

Then there was the game that's gone down in history as the greatest night at Loftus Road for a generation, when QPR beat Oldham in the play-off semi-final in May 2003. That night the TV cameras visibly shook on the TV gantry, as Paul Furlong scored the winner in a famous 1-0 victory. The celebrations after the goal nearly blew the roof off Loftus Road.

"As a fan growing up supporting Rangers, I can remember the glory years at Loftus Road. The Milk Cup semi-final against Liverpool in 1986 and FA Cup games, but I'd never experienced an atmosphere like the game against Oldham that night, nothing with that intensity. If I knew what that night was going to be like now, I'd have been so nervous before the match started. And I would definitely have been nervous watching.

"A packed house and the place was rocking. We were the best team on the night and we deserved to go through. But there was something special about the atmosphere at the club then. Olly said to me and Kev that, because we were fans of the club and all the fans knew how much the club meant to us, we were the link between the players and the fans.

"The fans knew we were giving everything for the club and we had a tremendous team spirit. I think that special bond we had at the club is missing this season. But I think what's happening at QPR now is what's happening to football in general.

"Fans think players are being overpaid and it looks like they're not giving 100 per cent for the club. And I suppose there's a bit of jealousy in there. But it's more to do with the fans thinking that if they had the same chance to play for their club, they would give absolutely everything. And I think you'll hear this being said across football."

Bircham insisted the current squad was thoroughly

professional, adding that they could hardly be blamed for this unflattering perception of the modern game. But he warned the board against any decisions that might alienate supporters. "The fans have been promised everything this season and nothing has really been delivered yet, and that seems to be how the fans are feeling.

"The club can't forget the fans who were there when they needed them the most, and the real fans are getting priced out now. It's getting like Chelsea, but at least Chelsea has got European football and Premier League football. But I think the board know that now. We're not that type of club. We're a working-class London club and you can't change the way a club is. That's what we've always been and that's what we are today. And I think the board are coming round to that way of thinking."

But QPR was also a club that could pull a big crowd when it wanted to. 30,000 turned up for the play-off final against Cardiff at the Millennium Stadium in May 2003, which QPR lost 1-0. "On a day like that you realise how big we really are. A club that's been supported by families through generations," says Bircham. "The kids came out, the granddads. It was a day I won't forget for a whole host of different reasons.

"I organised a coach for my family while I was staying in the hotel with the team. It must have been about 10 in the morning and my phone kept ringing and it was my dad. It was like something out of *Only Fools and Horses*: the coach had broken down and it was on fire. I said, 'What!' And he said again: the coach was on fire.

"I knew someone on Talksport and I think Five Live did the same, they put messages out that a coach had broken down on the motorway, and cars were pulling over picking up twos and threes and getting them to Cardiff. That was brilliant. I would have loved to have been there to see it.

"On the pitch during the game I get tunnel vision when I'm playing. So I didn't take in the size of the Rangers following there until afterwards. We were the better team. We should have won it. But after the game I found out that if we had won it, we'd have gone bust. The best thing that could have happened to us was to lose that final."

A reliable senior source at the club told Bircham that, because of contractual commitments involving some players, QPR would have had to pay their former clubs large sums of money if the club was promoted, in addition to player bonuses for gaining entry to the First Division. These extra costs would have been crippling. "We'd have had real problems," says Bircham. "The club was in so much debt, and it was paying off the ABC loan as well.

"Off-the-pitch stuff did affect me because my phone would be going non-stop, with family and friends wanting to know what was happening. But the game where it probably affected me most was the game of my life against Sheffield Wednesday at Hillsborough the following season, the game that got us automatically promoted.

"I remember the last month of that season, Neil Warnock kept ringing up and wanting me to sign for Sheffield United. He knew I was out of contract. I kept asking QPR about my contract, but they would say they couldn't deal with it until they knew which division we were playing in the following season.

"Eventually I found out that if the club didn't go up they wouldn't have been able to afford me. So not only was there the pressure of this vitally important final game of the season – beat Sheffield Wednesday away to get promoted – now I knew I was also playing to stay at the club. If we lost, my days at QPR were numbered.

"Added to that, I got a call on the Friday. Neil Warnock is going to the game at Sheffield Wednesday to watch me, just in case we don't win – and he's a Sheffield United fan and they hate him down there. But there was a good omen: the TV comedy series *My Family* was on, and in the show they're QPR fans, watching a game on the telly, and they're singing 'Come on You R's', so me and Kev thought, 'That's a good sign.'"

A 7,300-strong army of fans travelled to Hillsborough for the game. The task was simple: win against Sheffield Wednesday and Rangers were up in the automatic promotion position. It wouldn't matter what Bristol City did, who were lying in third place one point behind. The Rangers fans took over the Leppings Lane End and released thousands of blue and white balloons as the players came out on the pitch. Meanwhile, back at Loftus Road, 5,000 more fans were watching on a big screen as the game was shown live.

"When the game started, I'll always remember, in the first 10 minutes I was going up for a ball, I called it, and Clarke Carlisle came into the back of me and gave me the biggest dead leg. I thought, 'I don't believe it, I'm gone, and from one of my own players.' I still don't know how I played that entire game."

With the game still goalless, Bristol City went into a 2-0 lead against Blackpool after about 20 minutes at Ashton Gate. As it stood, they were up. "I still think it was out of order how Sheffield Wednesday kept flashing up the Bristol City score because Danny Wilson was their manager, and he was a Sheffield Wednesday legend.

"Their fans were cheering for Bristol City, but that spurred us on even more – not that we needed it, mind. That whole QPR end was enough to inspire anyone." And inspire it did. A first-half goal by Kevin Gallen on 35 minutes, followed by one from Paul Furlong just after the break and an own goal from Chris Carr in the 69th minute, sealed promotion. They went up in second place behind Plymouth Argyle, one point ahead of Bristol City in third.

"At the final whistle I remember just saying, 'I can stay, I can stay – fantastic!' I didn't have to leave QPR. Then I did a Pat Cash and ran straight into the crowd, because I knew exactly where my family were sitting. That was only the second time I saw my dad cry. The first time was at the FA Cup Semi-Final against West Brom. Now he was crying again because he knew how much this meant to me.

"Then I remember I was interviewed on the pitch and I was asked, 'What are you going to do now?' I thought the question meant how was I going to celebrate? So I said I was going to get pissed for a week. I think me, Gaz [Gareth Ainsworth] and Rolly [Martin Rowlands] didn't get changed out of our kits. Gaz still had his shin pads on, I'd taken mine off. Then we got onto a coach and went straight to a nightclub to celebrate. It just happened to be my missus' 30th birthday as well, so we hired a nightclub in London. The party wouldn't have been too great if we'd lost.

"And we *were* pissed for a week afterwards. That game at Hillsborough was like a final to us, there was more tension in that game than the play-off final the year before. It meant more because it felt like it was our last chance. If we'd not gone up then, I don't think we'd have won the play-offs and I think that team would have disbanded. I'd have had to go and I think Kev [Kevin Gallen] would have had to go. The emotions were relief and happiness. I think the fans knew it was our last chance too.

"I don't want to blow our own trumpet but we did the hard work then – and it *was* hard work, believe me. It must be like what Leeds and Leicester encounter now. Everywhere we went we'd get the highest attendances and everyone wanted to beat us. Opposing fans would chant, 'You're not famous anymore . . .' That team did so much work to get into the Championship and stay in the Championship as well, probably on one of the lowest budgets there. I think we did really well."

The severity of the financial problems occupying the club was obvious in the 2006-07 pre-season, one year before the takeover. "It was a shambles of a pre-season. On the Thursday before our first game of the season, against Burnley, I was going into training early about half past eight when I had a call from the physio, who said, 'You can't get in because the gates are locked.' I said, 'What?' and he repeated, 'You can't get in because the gates are locked.' We hadn't paid the bills. We were locked out."

Bircham was already en route when he received the call. When he arrived at the training ground to find out more about what was going on, his phone rang again. This time a member of the coaching staff told him that training was cancelled, because the training ground had been broken into. "And I said, 'Funnily enough, I'm outside it now and they're saying we can't go in because we haven't paid the bills.'

"We went up to Burnley thinking, 'Can you remember a worse preparation for a new season?' But that was the story back then. A couple of times coaches didn't turn up because we hadn't paid the bills and we had to quickly pay the coaches.

"All that was happening off the pitch did affect you as a player, always caring about what was happening at board level and afraid the club was going to go bust.

"Players wonder if they're going to get paid, but as a fan I was also watching a club in turmoil. What's going to happen to the club you and your family supported, that's been so important in your life?

"It's a very different club now, of course, with very rich people behind it. It's not the same QPR. The owners have put a lot of money into the club, and we probably didn't know how much debt there really was."

CHAPTER EIGHT

THE FIRST GAME of the post-Iain Dowie era was an away match, to high-flying Reading, third in the table and many experts' favourites for automatic promotion. Just one day before the encounter at the Madejski Stadium, Dowie was sacked by Flavio Briatore at the club's Harlington training ground and Gareth Ainsworth was installed as caretaker manager.

Ainsworth was QPR's longest-serving player. The gutsy, physical winger grew up in Blackburn, and – after spells with Preston, Lincoln, Wimbledon and Cardiff – joined Rangers in 2003. He helped the club get promoted from Division Two into what's now known as the Championship, during his first season.

In his very first game, he scored two goals in a 5-0 win over Blackpool. A few games later, he scored another couple against Rushden and Diamonds, both from about 35 yards out. He was always popular with the fans, because of his work rate and determination, and came second in the 2005-06 Player of the Year Awards.

As he says, "I'm proud of my involvement with QPR. Coming out of administration and being part of that, and being part of the story up to where the club is now. Every fan knows I've given nothing less than 100 per cent for the club. It's great when fans come up and talk to you in the street and thank you for all you've done, especially for coming though the tough times. I've never asked for thanks, but it makes me very proud to feel wanted by this club. A place I call 'my club' now, after all I've been through here."

When the current board took over, Ainsworth was relieved. "It was all about making the club secure. I went through troubled times when I was at Wimbledon as well. I know how difficult it was for us coming out of administration. Before the current owners came in, it was a worrying time for such a big club as this, with such a long history.

"Sometimes people say footballers are selfish and don't get involved in these sorts of things, but I realised during those difficult times that people at this club really cared about what was going to happen to QPR.

"Obviously, with the likes of Marc Bircham in the past and Lee Cook now, we're a club where lifelong fans become players and that doesn't happen too often. During the difficult periods, they really cared about the club and made us care as well and get more involved. When Flavio took over, it was about keeping that club together after all the turmoil we'd been through."

When Luigi De Canio was appointed first team coach in 2007, Ainsworth took his first tentative steps into coaching, helping the Italian who was struggling with the English language. In April 2008, he revealed to BBC Radio London that he was becoming De Canio's right-hand man: "I help out in team talks and get his messages across on the pitch and I'm happy to do that. I'm learning so much every day so hopefully I'll pick up a few badges and one day I'll be a coach or a manager even."

In May 2008, he accepted a player-coach role under Iain Dowie and, just five months later, was offered the full responsibility of becoming the gaffer. Known around Loftus Road as simply 'Gaz',

Ainsworth is one of the lads; he has also gained notoriety as a part-time rock singer in his band Dog Chewed the Handle.

But all the fans were now asking if he'd bitten off more than he could chew, in accepting this increasingly high-profile and highly-scrutinised post. The pace of events amazed everyone at the club.

Winger Lee Cook says, "The Swansea game, when we drew 0-0 and they didn't have a proper goalkeeper for most of the game, stood out for the owners. They felt they had to change things. But the players were disappointed when Iain left. Everyone got on with him and enjoyed working under him.

"It all came as a shock. We were at Harlington on the Friday morning and did training as usual. Flavio would often come down to watch us train, to have a chat with the boys and see how we are. Then Flavio said there was going to be a meeting with everybody in 10 minutes in the canteen. We just thought, 'What's this all about?'

"We came in from our wind-down for the meeting and he said to us that Iain was leaving and that he'd told him to clear all his stuff. Gareth was going to be taking charge for the foreseeable future. We all looked at each other.

"The team had just been picked, but Gareth said, 'Come in as usual. The team is going to change so everyone be ready to start tomorrow.' Everything happened really quickly. Nobody knew it was coming. People were saying in the media afterwards that there was an argument in the office or something, but we didn't see any of that.

"Apparently, there wasn't an argument. It was just a decision that had been made. Flavio had talked to the other owners about it. The press would have loved it if there was a row between Briatore and Dowie, but that wasn't true. It was a decision that was made. Managers change, that's just the way it is."

Ainsworth was thrown in at the deep end by the day's shocking events. As he explains, "It's never a nice moment when somebody gets released. We were upset but that decision was out of our hands. When they asked me to take the helm, I thought I'd give it 100 per cent. It was lucky that Iain had put such strong foundations in place since the start of the season.

"We had a lot of games in a small space of time, it was quick-fire. I just remember looking at the fixtures and we had Manchester United coming up in the Carling Cup, a real baptism of fire for me. I always knew it was going to be a temporary thing. But I was proud that I'd captained the club, been player-coach and was now caretaker manager at QPR. Not many people get to do that at a club."

But the scale of the task for Ainsworth was massive. He was put in charge just 24 hours before playing Reading away, who had a 100-per cent record at the Madejski Stadium. They had scored 21 goals in winning all six previous home games.

"In football, things change very quickly," he says. "People get transferred, people move on. Nothing surprises me now after 20 years in the game. I had just one day to get the team ready for that Reading game, which was a difficult situation for everyone concerned, but everyone responded fantastically."

Lee Cook saw Ainsworth's promotion as a turn-up for the books. He didn't know if he should call him Gaz or gaffer now, but stuck with the former. "I'd played with Gaz for three years when I was last with the club and I never saw him as a manager. But I learnt afterwards that he had been helping Luigi De Canio while I was at Fulham and, of course, he was part of the coaching set-up under Iain Dowie this season and really enjoyed it."

Ainsworth thought long and hard about how to best prepare the players for his first game in charge. "I made a decision not to write anything down before the match. Not to prepare a speech or anything like that. I just decided to go through the warm-up and go through all the preparations as usual. It was a big game on Sky, against one of the best teams in the league, away from home.

"I decided that, five minutes before they went out, I'd say whatever came into my mind at that moment. I'd speak honestly to them, from the heart. I remember the changing room going very quiet before I started talking, and I'm an emotional guy anyway before games. The message was go out there, give it your all and get the result, but I put that in my own words, how I would say it."

Lee Cook reveals that it was an emotional moment for the players as well. "His words to us before that Reading game were simple. He just said, 'Play your hearts out for me'. And we did."

Two of the three changes made by Ainsworth, from Dowie's line-up for his last game against Swansea, leapt out from the teamsheet. Samuel Di Carmine – a young Italian on loan from Fiorentina – replaced Dexter Blackstock for his first start in the team, while Daniel Parejo – the loan signing from Real Madrid who Briatore was instrumental in bringing to Loftus Road – returned to the side for the first time since September. These changes led to inevitable questions in the media about who suggested them: was it Briatore, Ainsworth or a combination of the two?

As the game turned out, Di Carmine impressed up front as the lone striker, before being subbed after an hour by Blackstock. The young Italian forced Reading keeper Marcus Hahnemann to parry his shot to safety in the first half, while Parejo tried to impose his passing game on midfield and had a volley on target. Akos Buzsaky had QPR's best chance, firing a 35-yard effort at Hahnemann after the break.

In defence, Damion Stewart was immense; Mikele Leigertwood, switched to right-back by Ainsworth, had a great game and Radek Cerny pulled off a fabulous save to keep out a header by Reading's Kalifa Cisse. The final score was 0-0.

Ainsworth was full of admiration for his players afterwards: "To have gone through what all the guys had gone through in the previous 24 hours, all that was happening off the pitch, and not necessarily to play for me but for the shirt and to wear that badge with pride, well, I was oozing pride myself. That day was the most emotional I'd ever felt in football."

Lee Cook confirmed how moved Ainsworth had been. "Gareth nearly cried afterwards. He was so full of pride that the players had performed like that for him."

In the post-match press conference, Ainsworth reiterated his pride in the stirring performance of his players. But reporters were far more interested in his relationship with Briatore. "I pick the team and I have the final input in who plays," he explained. "But Flavio is the biggest shareholder and he likes to have an active role in the team. He doesn't discuss strategy but he sees players and he says what he sees. He's a winner and he loves to be involved in sport. I'm happy to go along with that."

His opposing number, Reading boss Steve Coppell, also had to field questions on the managerial set-up at QPR. "Picking a football team is not a committee decision," he remarked. "I don't know what is going on at QPR but you can only read between the lines. I wouldn't tolerate that. If I didn't pick the team, what would I do?"

Ainsworth explains how he tried to distance himself as much as possible from this contentious issue on the day, to concentrate only on the match: "I had the final say on the team but I tried to keep away from all that on the day for the club's sake. I'm hopeful I could have picked any team on that day from the players on offer and done myself proud, but the press kept going on about this and I just wanted to do the job. Sometimes, there's too much speculation. The press can be your biggest fans or your biggest enemies. I just wanted to concentrate on the job in hand – the football."

Dexter Blackstock was one of the players dropped from the

starting line-up for the Reading game, with Samuel De Carmine chosen in his place. Blackstock reflected on the issue on his own website, *dexterblackstockofficialwebsite.com*: "There was a lot of talk about me being left on the bench the game after Iain Dowie got sacked. People said it was because Flavio wanted more of the new lads to play. To be honest, it didn't bother me at all. I've played some part in every game this season, whether it's been starting or from the bench. It's a squad game and you have to know that you're not going to play every minute of every match.

"Flavio's been really involved with the players since day one. He's always been in and around the dressing room and nothing's changed now that Gareth Ainsworth's in charge. Iain Dowie did well for us and I don't know the reason for him going, but managers come and go. It's part of the game now and you just have to get on with it."

Fans were pleased that Ainsworth was getting this chance to prove himself as a coach, even if the barrage of stories in the press were making them a little uncertain about his exact job description. Howard Prosser, former QPR fanzine editor, says, "I think he always had it in him to make that progression to the coaching side of the game and eventually become a manager. He's always been a fans' favourite. But there's a question about how much influence Briatore has on the team.

"In a way, if it is a kind of partnership, Gareth isn't going to miss this chance, even it isn't a typical manager's job, because I'm sure he feels delighted to be given this opportunity to show what he can do. I think we have to be happy with the situation. If we want this money invested in the club, now and in the future, and this is the deal, then we have to accept it and hope that Ainsworth is happy. And if we get results on the pitch, well, fans have accepted a lot of things this season that they're not used to. They've become resigned to the fact that this is the new QPR."

"Actually, funnily enough, if Briatore was to say, 'Right, I want a big role in managing this team and that's how it's going to be structured,' I'd say, 'Go on then, it's worth a go,'" claims broadcaster and lifelong Rangers fan Robert Elms. "We've had so many bad managers down the years, could he possibly be any worse than Alan Mullery – or any of the other clowns we've had for the job? We've had plenty of muppets. No, that doesn't bother me about Briatore if he wants to do that. The only problem then is who sacks him?

"But what do I think? I think we've got to let him have a go. Because I hope I'm a sane enough bloke to know what the alternatives are. The alternatives are Leyton Orient. And I'm more than happy to put up with the ride. After all I've put up with over the last 10 years, I can certainly put up with a slightly dictatorial Italian in blue glasses, shouting down team instructions from the directors' box.

"But I do think the current board has made some very bad PR mistakes. What they should have said is, 'We've sacked Dowie because we want to see good, flowing football – the Rangers way – and we know you do too.' Then everyone would have said great, fine. Welcome to W12. These are men who are not used to having to explain things to a fanbase. The Formula 1 fanbase is very different. It's not questioning, it's not there every week.

"People who follow a Formula 1 company don't feel like they own it, whereas Rangers fans feel like they do, though everyone knows of course that they don't. So I don't think you need to communicate with F1 fans in the same way.

"They don't have to communicate to us at all, of course. I don't know if he cares about that, I have no idea. But if they do want the fanbase on board, all they've got to do is get a bit better at talking to people, because fans will put up with anything really."

Lee Cook sheds light on the relationship between Briatore and the players, offering an insider's point of view: "First and foremost, you've got to impress the manager. And the manager has got to impress the board. But, as players, we've still got to impress Flavio as well. He comes to every game, home and away, when he's not out of the country with Formula One.

"Flavio likes to come into the changing rooms and have a chat with the players. They know that he's the main member of the board that gets involved with the club and they want to impress him. He's been a huge success at Formula One and won't stop until he gets that with QPR. But if there really was interference in team matters, it would directly affect the players and then people would definitely hear about it. He doesn't interfere with team selection, saying which players he doesn't want to play. That's solely down to the manager."

Gareth Ainsworth adds, "Flavio Briatore is a winner. He likes taking an interest in his club. He's put a lot of money in and it's fantastic to have such a winner in sport associated with this club. It's great to see him in his scarf in the directors' box. To have invested so much money into the club, he obviously wants to be involved.

"But there's no system to the way it works behind the scenes. He comes into the changing rooms, wishing the players all the best, but that's as far as it goes. He's just taking an interest in his club. And it's not after every game because he's got his other commitments."

Back on the pitch, the club was in the middle of a run of games that would have proven a stern test for the most experienced of managers, never mind a novice. After drawing with third-placed Reading away on the Saturday, QPR faced top-of-the-table Birmingham City at home the following Tuesday.

In the build-up to the game, Ainsworth offered a candid insight into how he was handling this new emotional rollercoaster, telling *The London Paper*: "It's given me a taste for it and I'd like to be a manager at some stage in my career. It was one of the proudest moments in my life, leading the team on Saturday. It's pretty manic with all the things to do, the phone calls I am getting.

"I have gone into it at full blast, just like I did as a player. I was reserve team manager which gave me a bit of grounding, but it still doesn't prepare you for taking the first team. Saturday was really emotional, powerful stuff. I'm not sure I was ready for it. It's totally different to being a player, where you can just concentrate on yourself and can afford to be a bit selfish."

The Reading game may have been an unforgettable experience for Ainsworth, but the Birmingham City match was even more intense. In atrocious weather conditions the atmosphere at Loftus Road was red-hot, and Ainsworth went as far as to admit afterwards, "I'll find it hard to have such an emotional experience as the Birmingham game in football ever again."

For many, this was the best game at Loftus Road during the season so far. In the midst of all the doubts and debate off the pitch about who was going be the long-term boss, or how that management process was going to work, the Rangers' performance was full of grit and determination, very much in the mould of their new caretaker manager, despite a disputed sending-off.

It was also the perfect match to re-ignite the passion of a lapsed QPR supporter. Graham Poll – who had been a professional referee for 27 years, from 1980 to 2007 – was attending Loftus Road again as a supporter for the first time in around 30 years. His dad had been a fan and took him to see the great side of the mid-70's that got so close to winning the league title in 1975-76.

"My favourite player back then was Dave Thomas," Poll says, "sprinting down the wings with his socks around his ankles –

which you wouldn't be able to do today, of course, because socks have to cover the shinpads nowadays. I used to love Phil Parkes in goal as well. He seemed an enormous player to me at the time. And then there was Stan Bowles, of course.

"If I was a referee back then, I would have thought it an absolute privilege to be on the pitch with a player as talented as Stan. That's what I always used to think about naturally talented players I refereed during my career, and I would have thought the same about him.

"Back then, QPR played football, got it down on the ground, speed down the wing, the right blend. They were a great side. But the successful eras of QPR weren't just about the likes of Rodney Marsh and Stan Bowles. There were hardworking players as well as skilful players. The blend was there.

"I was lucky that I supported QPR when they had such a great side. I started refereeing in about 1980 when I was 17 years old. I refereed on Saturdays, Sunday mornings and Sunday afternoons, matches with 22 hairy-arsed blokes. I remember one great occasion that summed up what it was like for me back then. This man ran onto the pitch with a magic sponge, and in his bucket, to keep them cold, were eight cans of lager. I was only aged about 17 at the time, and thought, 'I'm not sure that this is entirely legal.'

"But I think I've got to make it clear that I don't consider myself a real fan, like those who turn out to see QPR, or any team for that matter, through thick and thin. If you travel across the country for a night game, watch in the rain as they play rubbish but you cheer them on regardless, then you get into a car and travel back across the country again afterwards, then you're a real fan.

"I can recognise this as someone who's refereed and run lines at games across the country and witnessed this firsthand, but I'm not one of those people. Therefore I would say I'm not a fan, which derives from the word 'fanatic'. I'm a follower of QPR. I think there is a difference and wouldn't put myself into the same category as those fans, who I really respect. But if I do have one regret about the path I took, it's that I'm not one of those dedicated supporters of a team. You can see how much their club means to them."

For two or three years after he became a referee, Poll still had QPR in his blood. But as he got more involved he moved away from the club. He decided that, for a successful professional ref, it was the only way to go. As a result of his dedication, he was the man in the middle at two World Cups, a UEFA Cup Final, an FA Cup Final, 100 international matches and 329 Premiership clashes.

He adds: "The laws on being a referee and a fan are cloudy. It's left up to the judgement of the individual. You fill in a registration form each year. If you drink down the Dog and Duck every week then you shouldn't referee their pub team, as you know them. Referees put down that they can't referee a game because it's their team or, more normally, because that's where they live. I felt that by the time I was a referee – and I was refereeing at a national level in 1991 – I was far enough removed from being a fan to never disclose a team on my form.

"My dad was a park referee and a big QPR fan. He was always very supportive and tried to encourage me – apart from the time I ran the line in a QPR v Chelsea game in the late eighties, and I allowed what he claimed was a disallowed goal for offside by Kerry Dixon. I didn't give the offside and he didn't speak to me on the way home. The journey in the car was beautiful silence.

"He loved his Rangers and now my nephew, my dad's grandson, is also QPR through and through. I'm just waiting for the right time to get my eight-year-old to become a QPR fan. He supports the other team in west London right now, he loves Frank Lampard. When Frank leaves Chelsea . . . that will be my moment. I need QPR to be in the Premiership and for Frank to leave Chelsea, and the time will be right to change him over to Rangers."

When Birmingham City visited Loftus Road, Poll was joined for the match by his QPR-mad nephew, who has also had a referee's training. But the referee on the pitch, the controversial Stuart Attwell, proved a contentious figure at this volatile match. At 25, he was the youngest referee in Premier League history. Just the previous month he had allowed Reading the infamous 'ghost goal' at Watford, even though the ball clearly missed the net.

Attwell took centre stage at Loftus Road as a hard-fought contest with the league leaders was drifting towards halftime without a goal being scored. Mikele Leigertwood was challenging Lee Carsley in midfield and caught the Birmingham player. Without a moment's hesitation, Attwell brandished a red card to howls of protest from the crowd.

Then, just minutes later, former Italian international Damiano Tommasi was rampaging through midfield in an impressive first start in a Rangers shirt. He tangled with James McFadden, who the home fans believed struck out at Tommasi. But the next time the whistle was blown was for halftime and Attwell decided to book Tommasi for the incident.

The Rangers players were incensed. Martin Rowlands had to drag five of his team-mates away from the young referee. Gareth Ainsworth also marched on to confront Attwell, but was waved away by the official. As the players left the pitch, the home supporters were furious and the atmosphere was reaching boiling point.

As Poll says, "It was the red card which really did it. It was almost as if when the crowd got on his back – and I've been there – he said, 'Stuff you, I'll show you!' And with my QPR spectacles on, it almost appeared that decisions were going towards

Birmingham – you found yourself saying, 'Come off, ref! That didn't seem fair!'

"But when the tackle went in, my nephew, who's proper QPR and almost a qualified referee, went, 'Red card!' It was against one of his own players and I said, 'No, never.' He replied, 'You know nothing, you never have.'

"Of course, this all happened just before halftime, so I was walking around getting a drink at the break and people were saying to me, 'What's your bloody mate up to then, eh?' I was there as a QPR supporter, probably as frustrated as they were about the decision, but I was getting flack.

"When you're in the position of a referee making a decision like that, it's not a difficult decision to make if you are convinced you are right. You know it won't make you popular, but it's only difficult when the reaction of the players makes you think, 'Have I got that right or not?' When doubt comes into the equation."

The players had reacted badly to the sending-off, but only Attwell knew whether he was convinced in his own mind that he'd made the right call or not. For Gareth Ainsworth, the halftime speech was the biggest test of his leadership qualities so far. How could he inspire his 10-man team to victory?

"We all disagreed with the sending-off – 10,000 people in the stadium disagreed with it," Ainsworth says. "And here we were against the top team in the league, in the first game at home for the new caretaker manager, and it was being reported in the press that the club was in turmoil. It was so emotional, so intense that night. It's something I'll never forget.

"At halftime I wanted to go for it. I just remember going into the room for the coaches first and giving the players five minutes to themselves before going to them. Then I said, 'Everyone calm down. Nobody start ranting and raving at each other, we can win this if we play together.' We'd all had one hell of a first half and I wanted to give them belief that they could win this.

"We didn't want to waste energy arguing with the ref or each other. We just wanted to go out there and give it a right go. I decided to take Lee Cook off and play slightly differently. I was gutted for Cookie, we were team-mates not so long ago. We laugh about it now, but obviously whether it was the right or wrong decision depended on the result."

The second half was 45 minutes of sheer drama for the fans. "There was a magical atmosphere," Graham Poll says. "I told my nephew this is how it used to be at Loftus Road. A big club like Birmingham City at home, down to 10 men. Then Samuel Di Carmine scored a fantastic goal from 25 yards out to win the game 1-0.

"This match had everything. And it started to snow as well, which added to the electric atmosphere inside Loftus Road. Walking away after the final whistle towards White City, and with the snow still falling, took me back 30 years.

"When I got home I put on Sky Sports News. I looked at the red card incident again and actually thought that – because of the height of the tackle by Leigertwood, where he caught him and the risk of injury to the opponent – the red card was justified in the end. It's interesting. When I was in the crowd, I was looking for decisions to go QPR's way, which I suppose is understandable.

"All the headlines at the time were about Flavio. Did he get involved in picking the team or didn't he? I don't know if he did or not. I used to get very cross when people used to comment about me in the press when they didn't know me, so I won't do it now because I don't know the man.

"But in general terms, people should have defined roles in a football club and not interfere with each other. If you've got a football manager, let him do the job without anyone getting in his way. That's my opinion. What you definitely don't want is a director of football going around buying players that the manager doesn't want."

For vice-chairman Amit Bhatia the victory over Birmingham City was one of his highlights of the season. "We were down to 10 men, the snow, an unbelievable atmosphere and an unforgettable game. I have goosebumps just thinking about it."

The back-page headlines the next day had a similar upbeat feel to them. 'Flavio of the Month' declared *The Sun*. 'Perhaps Flavio Does Know What He's Doing' proclaimed the *Evening Standard*. The colourful chairman was still the focus of attention, even in victory.

The ongoing relationship between Briatore and Ainsworth was still the main topic of discussion at the post-match press conference after the Birmingham game, with team selection still top of the list of questions. "There will be discussions again through the parties and I will put my case forward for players," explained Ainsworth.

"Other people put the case forward for players and then the final input is mine on the pitch. People might have opened their eyes at the changes – wondered, 'Who? Why? When?' But the main thing is QPR won this game with 10 men. So whatever we've done is justified.

"The investment in this club is massive. We nearly went out of business, and people are interested in their investments, to know what's going on. I'm happy to be in those meetings and those discussions about the players. But on a Saturday, it's me in the dugout and I've got to get the 11 men going."

But the biggest test still lay ahead for the new caretaker manager: European and Premier League champions Manchester United at Old Trafford, in the fourth round of the Carling Cup.

The last round had been the highlight of Iain Dowie's reign, when he masterminded victory over Aston Villa at Villa Park.

Ainsworth had to try to emulate that achievement by locking horns with Sir Alex Ferguson, one of the greatest British managers of all time. The gulf in experience between both men was stark, best illustrated by the fact that Ainsworth was just a year old when Ferguson took charge of East Sterlingshire in 1974. Ferguson had 34 years in management, Ainsworth had just four games.

"I have tremendous respect for Man United," says Ainsworth. "And total respect for Sir Alex Ferguson. QPR is an ambitious club and this is where we want to be. It was a great taste for the fans, especially playing at Old Trafford. The club had been there in the 90's but had lost its way since then, with money problems, administration and relegation. We'd had a similar taste when we beat Aston Villa at Villa Park under Iain. It was like being a Premiership club again. And everyone has ambitions to go back there for real."

For the board at Loftus Road, this trip was a glimpse into the future. It was for major games like this that Briatore, Bernie Ecclestone and Lakshmi Mittal had invested their millions into QPR in the first place. This is where they wanted to be, playing clubs the size of Manchester United every season. Amit Bhatia even sat in the stand at Old Trafford instead of the directors' box, to properly enjoy the atmosphere among QPR's 6000-plus travelling support.

As did a sizeable contingent of Lee Cook's family and friends. He'd spent £720 on 20 tickets for them to watch the game, the first time he'd ever played against Manchester United. And for R's fans like Cook, the prospect of playing at Old Trafford brought back memories of the side that famously beat United in early 1992, at the 'New Year's Day Massacre'. As he says, "I remember when Dennis Bailey got that hat-trick in a 4-1 win. I was 10 years old and had been in hospital after an asthma attack. But I got my dad to pick me up and I was discharged early to get home and watch with my family."

Simon Barker played for QPR in this memorable game, one of the highlights of the late 80's/early 90's period when they were recognised as a top-flight outfit, twice finishing fifth in the league as London's top side. For the 1992 squad, with Gerry Francis in charge, there was nothing unusual about playing at the Theatre of Dreams. It was a fixture the players and fans looked forward to every season.

Manchester United went into this game in 1992 at the top of the league, and in the middle of a much-hyped sequence of matches against their nearest rivals, Leeds United. QPR were in the bottom half of the table, but were undefeated for six games.

"You've got to remember that we were a decent side then," Barker explains. "We had good players like David Bardsley and Clive Wilson as attacking fullbacks, Alan McDonald and Darren Peacock at centre-half, I was in midfield with Andy Sinton, Ray Wilkins and Ian Holloway, and upfront was Roy Wegerle. But it's Dennis Bailey that everyone remembers from that game, of course, because he scored that hat-trick.

"He came from nowhere and went back to nowhere, but he was a lovely lad with tremendous ability – quick, good in the air. But he didn't show it on a regular basis, that was his problem. I remember he was up against Steve Bruce and Gary Pallister that day and he was putting it through his legs and their legs, he was causing them all sorts of problems."

Amazingly, QPR were two up inside five minutes. They finished off United with two more goals in the second half. "At that time, I thought if we could afford one or two more players we could make a bid for Europe, and get into the top three or four places in the league.

"I was with QPR for 10 years and eight of those were in the top division. We finished above the likes of Arsenal, Chelsea and Tottenham on a regular basis. While our crowds weren't as big as theirs, everyone loved coming to our stadium at Loftus Road where the crowd was so close to the pitch. We played good football, but you took it for granted back then, that's just the way it was."

The game was screened live on terrestrial television on New Year's Day, and as the goals continued to hit the back of the net the players believed a victory was within their reach.

As Barker says, "We knew that most teams don't go to Old Trafford and win 4-1, but it didn't feel dreamlike to us. We were a decent club in good form at the time. We believed a win like this was in us. But we knew we'd done something special. And it's interesting how many people still say to me today, 'Did you play in that game?'

"A lot of fans remember it, from other teams as well as QPR. I think everyone enjoyed Man United getting beaten that day. It's gone down as one of those games that people of a certain age remember long after you've retired."

Reports in the QPR fanzines after the game were bursting with pride at the result. *In the Loft* carried this comment from an overjoyed fan: "My only regret was that like the majority of Rangers fans, I watched it on TV. I would have given anything to be there, it must have been a fantastic experience for the fans. I have no idea how many supporters we had there but they out-sang the United fans and had me on the brink of tears with their constant chanting. There is nothing I can say that could possibly explain how proud I feel to be a Rangers fan."

Barker's 10 years at QPR began in 1988 when he signed from Blackburn for £400,000. He made 315 appearances and scored 33 goals, transferring to Port Vale in 1998 where he finished his career. After retirement as a player he worked for the Professional Footballers Association, where he became a senior executive.

Barker observes how football has transformed since his days at QPR: "The game has changed a lot. It's about money now and having enough to move forward and buy the best players. And it's not just about millionaires anymore, it's about billionaires. When you heard about these people buying QPR, you thought, 'They've got a real chance to step back up a level.'

"If you look at Fulham, who I've always thought were a smaller club than QPR, they've been a Premier League club for a long time now and it needed a multimillionaire to get them there. I think it's harder now to bridge that gap between the Championship and the Premier League than it was when Fulham did it. It doesn't happen overnight. I hope the new owners are going to build something at QPR and take their time."

But Barker admits he'd grown increasingly concerned about the constant flow of stories in the press, and whether the right long-term decisions were being made to build the club's future.

"I'm not sure anything is going to happen with a short-term fix. I don't want to view this whole situation through rose-tinted spectacles. In my day, QPR had to sell a player every couple of years to balance the books. We sold Darren Peacock and Andy Sinton for good money. But the game's just moved more and more towards money now – and is it healthier for that? I'm not so sure. I'm worried about debts that some clubs are building.

"But the truth of the matter is that if a club like QPR has all this money behind it, and the board use it in the right way and build for the long-term future, then they've got a chance."

In the end, a repeat of the shock victory at Old Trafford in 1992 was beyond the current QPR side. But they put up a gallant display, holding out until the 76th minute when Carlos Tevez converted a penalty to seal a 1-0 win for United.

As Gareth Ainsworth says, “For those 76 minutes, the performance was fantastic. We battled hard and Radek Cerny pulled off some fantastic saves. We had 11 determined guys, who defended with their lives for QPR, and until the last 15 minutes we held off the European champions.”

Ainsworth had done little wrong during his short spell in charge. He’d lost just one of his five league games before the Manchester United defeat. But then QPR lost at home to Burnley on the following Saturday, which would be his last game as caretaker manager.

Just one week after the visit to Old Trafford, *The Sun* revealed that Paulo Sousa was Flavio Briatore’s choice as the next first team coach at QPR. Ainsworth would return to his old position of player-coach.

“I always knew it was going to be temporary, just a caretaker position,” Ainsworth says. “Flavio said to me he was going to give Paulo Sousa the job and thanks for all I’d done. That was it really. I half expected it and I’d had a fantastic time in charge. With Paulo coming in, my only thought now was what could I do to make QPR successful? It was great to meet him, a proven winner on the pitch, and I was going to help him in whatever way I could.”

Sousa had a celebrated career as a player and was a member of Portugal’s famous ‘Golden Generation’, the highly respected squad that won the 1989 World Youth Championship and then became one of the most accomplished national sides in world football. He went on to win 51 caps, playing as a defensive midfielder alongside the creative flair of Luis Figo and Rui Costa.

After a successful domestic career for Benfica and Sporting Lisbon, he achieved a unique double by becoming the only player to ever win a Champions League medal in consecutive seasons, but with two different teams. He helped Italian giants Juventus to Europe's premiere trophy in 1996 and then repeated the feat with German team Borussia Dortmund a year later.

His playing career also took him to Inter in Serie A. But Sousa suffered several serious injuries over the years and was forced to retire, aged only 31. He began a career in coaching by joining the staff of the Portuguese national team, overseeing the development of the under-15's.

In the summer of 2008 he was made assistant to national coach Carlos Queiroz, but was tempted by Flavio Briatore to move to Loftus Road just a few months later. The chairman had sought the advice of Fabio Capello, Luiz Felipe Scolari and Jose Mourinho, among others, before approaching Sousa. They gave him a glowing reference.

Nine days after the game at Old Trafford, Briatore introduced Sousa to the squad as their new first team coach, declaring that a fresh chapter would begin with the game away at Watford two days later. But Sousa's first glimpse of his new players in action must have been a bit of a culture shock. Quite what he thought as he sat in the stands at Vicarage Road, observing the shocking 3-0 defeat, is hard to imagine.

Having just arrived at QPR he wanted to take a backseat for his first game as boss, leaving Ainsworth in charge on the day. He must have run out of ink in making notes on potential improvements, because the performance at Watford was one of the worst of the season.

On this evidence there was plenty that had to be put right before QPR became play-off contenders. But was he the man to turn things around on the pitch? Was he the star name who would work best with the club's equally high-profile owners?

And could he bring his golden touch to the current squad of players, emulating the most successful eras of QPR's past?

OCTOBER/NOVEMBER

GARETH AINSWORTH AS CARETAKER MANAGER

Reading 0-0 QPR
25th October, 2008
Attendance: 20,571
Visiting QPR fans: 2,236
Table: 9th with 19 points

QPR 1-0 Birmingham
28th October, 2008
Attendance: 13,594
Scorer: Di Carmine
Sent off: Leigertwood
Table: 7th with 22 points

Ipswich 2-0 QPR
1st November, 2008
Attendance: 20,966
Visiting QPR fans: 1,169
Table: 7th with 22 points

QPR 1-0 Cardiff
8th November, 2008
Attendance: 13,347
Scorer: Mahon
Table: 7th with 25 points

Man United 1-0 QPR (Carling Cup R4)
11th November, 2008
Attendance: 62,539
Visiting QPR fans: 6,295

QPR 1-2 Burnley
15th November, 2008
Attendance: 13,226
Scorer: Blackstock
Table: 10th with 25 points

Watford 3-0 QPR
22nd November, 2008
Attendance: 16,201
Visiting QPR fans: 2,314
Table: 12th with 25 points
(Ainsworth in charge on matchday, Sousa observing in stand)

CHAPTER NINE

THE NUMBER 10 shirt has an almost mythical presence down at Loftus Road. It has always been worn by the team's playmaker, the entertainer who helped forge the Rangers style of attacking football with skill and flair.

In the past it had been worn by terrace legends like Roy Wegerle, Simon Stainrod, Tony Currie, John Byrne and Kevin Gallen; today, the tradition is continued by Akos Buzsaky, the team's current playmaker.

The stated aim of the new owners was to build a team that could compete in the Premiership again, perhaps emulating and even surpassing former glories. Two players personify the better times in QPR's history, both famous wearers of the Number 10 shirt: Rodney Marsh and Stan Bowles, the most popular players in the history of the club, core players in the fantastic sides of the late 60's and mid-70's.

In the next chapter Stan Bowles will relive his period in the Number 10 shirt, but first we'll hear from Rodney Marsh:

"I was a maverick when I played football. Everything I did, I did off the cuff – other than playing for England, which I hated because it was all so structured and rigid. I always played for the benefit of my team, but played it as I saw it.

"Sometimes when I did outrageous things, the opposing defenders and goalkeeper would clap. I remember once, I chipped the Middlesbrough goalkeeper from the right-hand side, 25 yards out. The ball hit the inside of the left post, bounced along the line and went in off the other post. And the goalkeeper clapped."

Marsh was signed by Alec Stock in March 1966 from Fulham for £15,000, where he was top scorer the previous season with 18 goals. He joined QPR when they were playing in the third division. "It became a proper football club when I joined it, and that's down to Jim Gregory becoming chairman. Before that QPR was a small club in west London that a few people cared about.

"Brentford in those days was probably a bigger club. When I first signed from Fulham, I'd left behind a club in the old first division with Johnny Haynes as captain. I thought, 'What have I let myself in for here?' but within two years I'd played for Young England, achieved promotion into the top division, scored 44 goals in one season, and won a League Cup medal.

"Alec Stock was a manager who understood me. 'Be a free player, Rodney,' he would say. 'Play as you like, play off the cuff. The only thing I ask is that you produce it on the day.' And I think I did that for him."

The highlight of his period in the number 10 shirt was the League Cup Final victory over West Bromwich Albion on 4 March 1967, the only major silverware the club had ever won. From being two down at halftime against a top first division side, QPR, who were two divisions lower, won 3-2 in front of 97,952 fans at Wembley Stadium.

"I think the 1967 team was the best QPR team ever. It could go away from home and beat teams 7-1. We went unbeaten for ages, a great bunch of lads who enjoyed playing together. And it was nearly always the same 11 playing. When I think of the teams I've played in – I've played for England and for Manchester City with the likes of Colin Bell and Mike Summerbee – that QPR team was the best ever. Alec Stock deserves all the praise for that. He was a very disciplined and structured man.

"I'll always remember, he called me into his office one day and said to me, 'Rodney, at the start of each season, I write down my best 11 players onto a piece of paper, which I put away in the drawer of my desk. Now, during the season plenty of players may come and go, but at the end of the season that 11 players I put on that piece of paper will still be my best 11, I can assure you of that.' He was a one-off, he really was, and I had total respect for him."

The League Cup Final victory is a legendary match in the history of the club, but the night before also became the stuff of legend for the players themselves. "We had a player called Bobby Keetch. He wasn't a first-team player. He was reserve team and on the bench. But he was a real character, a lovely, lovely man. He's dead now, sadly.

"Bobby was a bit of a wide boy back then. He loved the girls and champagne, he fitted in perfectly with QPR in those days. But he was also a gambler. Now you've got to remember this cup final was the equivalent of Liverpool v Swindon today. West Brom were a top club in the top division, we were in the third division. We didn't even expect to win ourselves, in all honesty.

"A couple of days before the game, Alec Stock said that Jim Gregory had got us into a hotel the night before the game, so that we could relax. Keetchy asked where it was and it was in Mayfair. Well, Keetchy burst out laughing because he knew we'd be surrounded by all the trouble in the West End.

"And then Alec Stock said, 'Oh, by the way, you'll be wearing all-white strips.' We thought, 'What?' We'd never worn white before, ever. Now we were going to play at Wembley looking like Real Madrid. Well, when we wore the strips we went onto the pitch feeling 10 feet tall. But, before the match, Keetchy put a bet of £200 on West Brom to win, they were odds on.

"So the night before the game, we're staying in Mayfair. We get to the hotel about 7pm and have an evening meal. Then, at about 10pm, Keetchy starts phoning around. He'd been out for a few drinks because he's not playing, he's on the bench. There was a card game in Room 41 or something – 'Anybody want to come up for a game of cards?'

"There were about nine of us from the cup final squad up there. There was champagne and cards and we were all playing poker. It was about three in the morning when it all ended. Then Keetchy doubled the bet on West Brom the next morning!

"There was an amazing bond in that team. Mark Lazarus on the wing summed up that team ethic on the pitch, so did Les Allen (Clive Allen's dad), who I played alongside upfront, one of the most underrated players to ever play the game.

"Then we had Mike Keen and Keith Sanderson in midfield, who ran themselves into the ground for the team and allowed the rest of us to play. It was all lads together – all for one and one for all – having a laugh together and playing to win together.

"I played the League Cup Final itself in a bit of a fog. I only wish that every footballer and football fan had the opportunity just once to play at Wembley and score a goal. The high you get from that is like nothing else you'll experience in your life. It was just amazing.

"All your senses are heightened, the smell of the turf, the colours seem brighter, it was just as if everything appeared in Technicolor by the experience of playing at Wembley on that day. The way I played the game, I didn't know what I was doing next most of the time. That's why defenders didn't know either. They used to just try to chop me down. I was an instinctive footballer."

During the first half, West Brom were dominant while Rangers struggled and the West Midlanders had a deserved 0-2 lead at halftime. But the second half saw a famous transformation. Rangers were a different team, attacking their opponents' goal; in the 63rd minute Roger Morgan headed home the first, and then, in the 75th minute, Marsh scored a stunning second, still rated as one of the great Wembley goals.

"When I scored the equaliser, I was about 35 or 40 yards out when Mike Keen drove the ball into me," Marsh explains. "I controlled it, then spun off to my left looking for a pass really. I was wandering across the pitch looking for someone to pass to, and I managed to go past three or four players without even knowing I was doing it.

"By this time, I was about 25 yards out and it just opened out for me to hit it. I clearly remember how pure the strike was, and it went in off the inside of the post. The ball was past the goalkeeper before he'd even moved because I struck it so sweetly. Other times I could have scuffed it, but not that day."

With the score at 2-2, and with just nine minutes to go, there was a mistake in the West Brom defence. Ron Hunt had a chance to score, but the goalkeeper saved it; the ball escaped free to Mark Lazarus, who tapped in the easy winner for a truly famous 3-2 victory.

"It was the most important game of my life," reveals Marsh. "It established QPR as a real, proper football club, and the club has moved on since that day. But that was the launch pad that made QPR the respected club they are today. It was a special day for the fans too. 7,000 people marched from Shepherds Bush to Wembley carrying a coffin with 'WBA RIP' on it.

"We used to mix with the fans in those days and there were some really interesting characters. A couple of the fans were bookmakers. A couple were really serious villains, proper hard cases, though I won't give any names of course, and they just loved me. When I read the stories of what players get chastised for in the press today, I have to smile.

"Back then, I remember one occasion when we were coming back from a game, all sitting in the same train carriage, and one of these villains threw someone off the train. This guy had been giving me and a few of the lads a bit of gob, so he got thrown out the carriage door! We were going through Watford Junction at the time so I don't think the train was going very quick, but we were gobsmacked. Something like that happening is unimaginable today, but the profile of the game was different back then."

One of the lasting impressions from the League Cup Final victory was hearing the chant of "Rod-nee, Rod-nee . . ." echoing around Wembley. It became famous down at Loftus Road, now regarded as one of the first-ever chants by fans of a player's name – though it had less than glamorous origins:

"What happened was, in my first game for QPR, we played away to Peterborough and I had a really terrible game, I was useless. And the Peterborough fans started singing, 'Rod-nee,' in a camp, piss-take way. Then we came back home to Loftus Road and we were playing Millwall, I think, and they started doing the same thing, singing, 'Rod-nee,' in the same piss-take way.

"But we beat them 6-1 and I scored three, if I remember correctly. Then the QPR fans started chanting in a really manly way, 'Rod-nee!!! . . . Rod-nee!!!' So they in fact reclaimed the chant, and that's where the 'Rod-nee' chant came from. It stuck."

The chant was of great interest to a young musician who'd just started following QPR and was immediately hooked on the atmosphere at Loftus Road, as the 60's came to an end and the 70's began. Michael Nyman was to become one of the country's leading composers, best known for the memorable soundtrack to the Oscar-winning 1993 film *The Piano*. (The soundtrack album sold more than three million copies.) But back in the 1971-72 season, he was a young man in his twenties who had recently moved to Ladbroke Grove, west London, just a couple of miles away from Loftus Road.

One Saturday afternoon he was walking along Portobello Road, around the corner from his new home, with a friend called Gavin Bryars who was also a composer.

"He said, 'What are you doing this afternoon?'" explains Michael. "I said, 'Nothing,' and he said, 'Do you want to see QPR?' 'Where do they play?' I asked. 'A 15-minute walk away,' he replied. He was a fan and had been going for years. Another friend of mine had been going since his dad took him in 1949.

"So I said I was free that afternoon, and I was hooked from that day on – the quality of the football, the feel of the stadium, the whole thing of being at a live match. It was the first time I'd gone to a match since I was seven. I was brought up in a northeast London family of Spurs fans. But the pull of Rodney Marsh and the quality of the football changed all that. I was QPR from that moment on, to the point that I planned my whole week around seeing the next match.

"I'd always be reading the reports in Saturday papers, Sunday papers and Monday papers. I was in my twenties and, back then, being a football fan wasn't quite the trendy thing it is now for media people. It was coming out of leftfield really. No one was really interested in live football then."

Nyman remembers once doing a concert in Brussels, Belgium, trying to catch a QPR result by listening to a radio under the piano. He also worked as a journalist on *The Spectator*. "I used to think, 'Why can't I be Michael Whale?' A journalist writing in the QPR programme, his job sounded great.

"But I believe that one of the best bits of writing about football was by a friend of mine, a musician called John Tilbury. I got *Vogue* to commission John to write about his experiences at QPR. It was very interesting." Applying musical theory to what they both heard being sung on the terraces, it analysed the differences in the 'Rod-nee' chant depending on whether the club was winning or losing. When winning, it was in a major chord and when losing in a minor, going from a G to an E.

Tilbury, a respected improvisational pianist, even incorporated the 'Rod-nee' chant into a piece of music he arranged for a concert at the South Bank Centre. A music reviewer wrote in *The Times* afterwards, "Did Marsh actually score during the Cardew 'Treatise' or was I hallucinating?" ('The Treatise', by avant-garde composer Cornelius Cardew, was the music performed during the concert.)

As Nyman explains: "I was a season ticket holder in the South Africa Road stand back then. But there wasn't any glamour around the club. It wasn't like Chelsea in the early 70's. Instead, we had our glamour on the pitch, with players like Rodney and then Stan Bowles a couple of years later. And that Rodney chant was one of the things that made Loftus Road special back then."

When Marsh was told that the chant had been analysed in this way by Nyman and his musical friends on the terraces, he was taken aback. "I can feel the hairs standing up on the back of my neck. That's amazing isn't it? I'd never expect anything like that to happen. But I've been told that chant has become quite famous because it was unique and not based on a well-known song or anything.

"I had some fantastic times at Rangers and some amazing games. My favourite games include one against Tranmere at Loftus Road. I couldn't do a thing wrong that day. Back heels, flicks . . . The most outrageous things came off for me. I think I scored four that day.

"Another game I played around that time, after the Cup Final in 1967, was against Bournemouth at Loftus Road. I'd read a story in the paper in which Bill Nicholson, who was manager of Spurs, said he liked to come down to Loftus Road in his spare time because he loved to watch Rodney Marsh play football, and he was at this game.

"So I did a trick that I'd tried before but it had never quite come off. I used to drag the ball from my right foot to my left foot, and then back to my right foot, and as the defender moved across me, I'd drive the ball between his legs.

"Now, when I hit the ball, it was always my aim to hit the underside of the crossbar on the way into the goal. On this occasion I did manage to hit the bar, but the ball bounced out again. It didn't go into the net. If it had gone in, they wouldn't have been able to stop me celebrating.

"I tried the same trick in a game against Birmingham City, which is quite famous now because it was caught on camera by LWT's *The Big Match* and I scored a hat-trick. But this time, when I shot it through the defender's legs I didn't strike the ball properly. It went into the bottom corner of the net and didn't get near the crossbar. I scored in that game but didn't pull the trick off properly, so I was a bit disappointed."

Another young QPR fan of the time, standing on the terraces at Loftus Road and marvelling at Rodney's skills, would also attain a high profile later in life. The story of Alan Johnson MP is an inspirational one. A young working-class lad from Notting Hill, west London, who loved watching QPR, he would one day climb the political ladder to become one of the most powerful politicians in the land.

Johnson, born in 1950, grew up in a Notting Hill very different to the fashionable and exclusive enclave it became in the 90's. Back in the 50's, the area became synonymous with slum landlords and inner-city deprivation.

"Because you were born in Notting Hill, QPR was automatically your team," Johnson said. "My first match was in 1958, when I was eight years of age, and I remember who it was against. I went down to Loftus Road with a mate to see QPR versus Bournemouth and Boscombe Athletic." This club became known as AFC Bournemouth in 1971.

Johnson had many obstacles to overcome in his early life. He was orphaned at the age of 12, when his mother died, and faced going into a Barnarado's home until his elder sister, Linda, impressed council officials with her maturity. The pair of them were allowed to share a council maisonette in Battersea, south London, even though she was just 15.

Johnson, who passed his 11-plus and earned a place at Sloane Grammer School in Chelsea, left school early without a single O-level. After stacking shelves at Tesco, he moved in 1969 to a council estate called the Britwell in Slough, Berkshire, and worked as a postman during the 70's.

"I lived in Slough for 19 years in this big council estate. A lot of west London people moved out there at the time to this estate. We used to all come into town to watch Rangers."

Johnson became a union activist, acquired academic qualifications in his twenties and rose through the ranks of the National Union of Communication Workers to become general secretary. A career in politics beckoned and he was elected as a Member of Parliament in 1997.

In 2006 he was appointed Education Secretary in Tony Blair's government, and Gordon Brown made him Health Secretary when he became Prime Minister a year later. But political experts were predicting greater things still for Johnson. At the beginning of 2009 he was being tipped as a future leader of the Labour Party and a potential Prime Minister himself one day. A lifelong QPR fan in 10 Downing Street seemed a genuine possibility.

Not bad for a lad from humble west London beginnings, who displayed a passion for his team that will resonate with boys from all generations. It was the League Cup-winning side of the 60's that truly captured his imagination.

"Something really special happened when they signed Rodney Marsh. They had a good goal-scoring team even before Rodney arrived. Players like Mike Lazarus and Tony Ingham, but then you had Rodney's arrival and everything stepped up a level.

"He's one of my heroes," says Johnson. "The entrance money was worth it just to see Rodney in the pre-match kickabout. He used to juggle oranges sometimes, the skills he had and watching him do it in a match were just amazing.

"He doesn't get the credit he deserves because he spent so long with us in the lower divisions and the matches weren't filmed in those days. No one saw those tricks that Rodney did. After he did something – it didn't matter if Rangers had lost – the crowd would just stand there, not believing what they'd seen.

"I especially remember a couple of occasions with Rodney. He ran half the pitch against Bristol City once, in the second division, treating the ball like a snooker ball. If you can imagine a snooker ball on a snooker table, you can clip it so that it shoots forwards on the table then back again like it's on a piece of elastic. Well, he was doing this with a football at his feet, the length of the pitch, making an absolute mockery of defenders.

"They didn't know what was going on. They'd never seen anyone do that. Then he took a shot and it went an inch over the bar. Other times, if he was waiting for a corner, he'd pick up someone's *Daily Mirror* and lean against the goalpost and start reading it while he was waiting for the corner to come over.

"And Marsh was a big guy, but he had that amazing touch. Then we had that fantastic season when we won the League Cup. We were a romantic team. People talk about West Ham being 'the academy' – well, we were in a lower division but we had great ball players.

"That QPR Number 10 shirt – that passed from Marsh to Stan Bowles to Tony Currie to Simon Stainrod to Roy Wegerle – that meant something and it really has created a romance around the club. I think that may be why we've got the interest in the club now.

"I remember when Rodney left, there was a black-tinged programme for the game directly after he'd gone. Nowadays, when someone leaves, fans say, 'You this or you that . . .' But when Marsh left, everyone was just saying thanks for the memories. We were in the second division but everyone was proud that he was going onto that bigger stage with Man City, who were top of the league then. I was really sorry to see him go but I wished him well.

"Everyone has their special era and the Rodney era was mine, when we went from being a nothing third division side to being a side that mattered in London. Brentford never did it. You've got to remember, we were a Bury or a Hartlepool in the shadow of Fulham and Chelsea at the time, but we were an ambitious club with a bit of bravado."

An ambitious club in the shadow of Chelsea and Fulham – that sounds familiar . . .

Leaving QPR was a wrench for Rodney Marsh, who joined Manchester City in March 1972. The two-year contract he signed with QPR in the summer of 1970 had contained the condition that, if the club failed to be promoted the following season, he could be sold to another. Tottenham were interested, but he ended up at Maine Road.

The night before he signed, he had second thoughts. He was drunk and rang chairman Jim Gregory, saying that he wasn't sure he was doing the right thing. But Gregory, a father-figure to

Marsh during his years at Rangers, replied that it was too late to halt the transfer.

"I felt terrible when I left QPR," recalls Marsh. "I'd travelled with the team from the third division to the first, and won the League Cup. But it was time for me to move on to a bigger club and Manchester City was the top club then. The transfer was £200,000, a record at the time. QPR bought five players with that money, and one of them was Stan Bowles. So, as it turned out, it was good business for me and for the club."

In 242 appearances for QPR Marsh scored 134 goals. After leaving, his career took him to Manchester City, back to Fulham with George Best briefly in the mid-70's, and famously to Tampa Bay Rowdies in Florida, USA. He was one of the British pioneers of the North American Soccer League and became chief executive of the Rowdies after retiring.

It was while he held this post that he got a call out of the blue in 1994, from Richard Thompson, QPR's chairman at the time. Marsh had been returning to the UK occasionally in the early 90's to make popular after-dinner speeches with Best, which turned into a touring show.

"I was heavily criticised for what happened at QPR at the time," Marsh says. "I got a call from Richard Thompson and he said, 'I want to have a chat with you.' He asked me my opinion on how to take QPR to the next level. Around that time, they were sixth or seventh in the league, they had a terrific team, with the likes of Les Ferdinand. And he wanted to know my opinion on how the club could move forward."

Gerry Francis was the manager at the time, and it seems he wasn't aware of a meeting between Marsh and Thompson. "We had a long lunch and I told him what I thought: that QPR were very close to being a top, top football team. I thought QPR were three players short of being that team. I'd seen them play six times that season and I identified the positions and the players.

"My position would have been chief executive. Gerry Francis would still be the manager, and I said, 'He's got to do what he's got to do.' I wouldn't interfere with that. I was never going to be manager. I've never wanted to be one. My role would have been chief executive, like you get in America.

"They oversee marketing, promotions, the type of players a club would sign. They know what the club can and can't afford. Basically, they add a new dimension to the club. And I've got to be clear about this: it's not a director of football position. A chief executive oversees the whole club. A good example would be what Niall Quinn is doing at Sunderland.

"I met Richard Thompson three times and we talked it through. I was told I'd get an annual salary to be chief executive of QPR. I said that would involve me moving back from America. I wouldn't want to do it half-arsed; I'd want to do it properly. He said, 'I'd like you to be chief executive of the football club.' I said, 'Let me think about it.' It was a big move for me. QPR were playing on the Tuesday night, I was invited along to the game and I was told Terry Venables was going to be there.

"On the Monday evening, I get a call from someone on *The Sun* and I'm told that they're running this story that I'm taking control at QPR. I told him, 'You've got this all wrong,' and said I've got no comment. He said, 'So you're not confirming or denying the story?' And I repeated, 'No comment,' and hung up on the guy.

"The following morning, it's all over *The Sun*'s back page with quotes from sources but no quotes from me. I still don't know how they got the story, whether it came from someone inside the club or if it was just great journalism getting to hear about it.

"Anyway, Gerry Francis was enormously pissed off about it. I went along to the game and it was a Sky match so the cameras were everywhere. I was given a QPR scarf and a seat beside Terry Venables and I was thinking, 'Have I been set up here?' It was like something out of a Monty Python sketch. Next thing, Gerry's resigned, thinking that I've come in behind his back. But nothing could have been further from the truth. I'd never wanted to manage or coach in England.

"Two days later I had a meeting scheduled with Richard Thompson. He brought me in on a conference call with his father, who I think was in Barbados or somewhere at the time. They said, 'Everything has changed now. Gerry Francis has resigned. It's a completely different situation.'

"'But you've offered me a job,' I said. 'I've been talking to my family about leaving America. If everything has changed now, we have to work out an arrangement,' and we went round and round, and they settled an amount of money with me eventually for my services up to that date, which I was happy with."

In parallel to the first full season of Flavio Briatore's leadership, chairman Richard Thompson was unpopular with a section of the fans. He was perceived by them as distant, uninterested in their concerns and intent on running the club solely as a profitable business.

In May 1996, the Thompson family announced their intention to sell the club. Three months later, media tycoon Chris Wright – a Rangers fan for 20 years – bought it. "Richard Thompson lost faith in the club because of the supporters and the way they treated him," Marsh says. "I rang him up and he said, 'That's it, I've had enough. I'm leaving.' Then Chris Wright took over, who was useless. The philosophy of the football club was all wrong."

When Thompson was chairman, Marsh insists, the steady decline of the club into the third tier of British football and financial instability did not seem possible. All he could see was potential success but, he claims, QPR's collapse would coincide with Thompson leaving and Wright taking over.

"In 2001, I said QPR could end up in the Conference and I got vilified for it," Marsh said. "Four or five years later, I got hundreds of fans emailing me and apologising. You can have the best things off the pitch – the best suites for sponsors, the best boxes, the best scoreboards and the most attractive cheerleaders. But the most important thing is the team on the pitch. That will never, ever change.

"QPR under Chris Wright completely got that wrong. If you look at the QPR players at the time, some of them looked like Sunday league pub players. I'm not going to slag off individual players, I would never do that, but I went to a couple of games back then, and some of the players looked like they were straight out of a crap Dog and Fox pub side.

"In the boxes you had all the showbiz types having champagne. It was ridiculous. If I was chief executive, it would have been very different. The club would have kicked on. We would have signed those three players. I would have earmarked the positions. And this isn't nuclear physics. If you look at the best teams in the world, every team has a dominant central midfield player – for example, Patrick Vieira, Roy Keane, Steven Gerrard and Frank Lampard. QPR was short of that player.

"The team could score goals, get the ball wide, they had those kinds of players in the team. But in my opinion they needed a quality general in midfield, a power player. It comes back to this point about the philosophy, that the team on the pitch is the most important thing. That's the product. In America, it would be perceived as selling a product. I don't think Chris Wright had his philosophy right."

As financial problems nearly swallowed up the club during the years that followed, Marsh was approached to front a consortium of wealthy men who didn't seem particularly interested in football. "They wanted to buy QPR and turn Loftus Road into a high-rise development, moving QPR's stadium out to near Heathrow Airport where they owned a load of land. But the plan didn't get off the ground. I didn't like them. They were all a bit too much in your face."

Eventually, the new owners completed their takeover of the club and the future looked a whole lot healthier. "At the start of this season, I said, 'I haven't been as excited about QPR as I am now for a very, very long time.' If you take the components of what it is to be successful, QPR have those components right now.

"QPR obviously has the money behind it with the new owners, but it's not just about that. When I went down there this season there was a fresh coat of paint everywhere, a new feeling around the place and a new logo, which I like by the way. I know it's come in for criticism from some quarters, but I like it. And all this combined was giving me the distinct impression that everyone thought the club had turned a corner. There was a sense of optimism around the place.

"But the question I would have is about the decision-making process in moving forward. In the football business, the customers are the fans. The product is the team on the pitch. In the past, there have been many examples of clubs getting this balance wrong and coming unstuck.

"Flavio Briatore seems to be the man calling the shots at QPR now, he's making the decisions. And he has to have a philosophy the staff and board of directors understand and can deal with, so when he says something the club does it. And this includes the manager, coaches, everyone, they all have to buy into the chief executive's philosophy: 'This is what we're doing and this is how we're going to do it.'

"When I was chief executive of Tampa we had a three-year

plan, a business model if you like. If I was in control of QPR now, I would establish two or three things, drawing on what we did at Tampa. I would introduce an annual summer camp, and this would be somewhere the players would also go to talk to these youngsters about football and teach them skills. Over a two-week period you would bring in 400 or 500 kids, who would learn about the game from professional players and coaches.

"It gives you a chance to discover good young talent and the PR would be tremendous. At the end of the camp, the kids would get a poster, a t-shirt and a QPR baseball cap, and then you've got yourself a young QPR fan going around town in his t-shirt and baseball cap. I did this with Tampa in the early 80's, and at one stage we had 1900 kids at our summer camp over a 13-week period. It was a money-maker and fantastic PR. Afterwards, there were kids everywhere walking around town wearing Tampa Bay Rowdies t-shirts. Could you imagine seeing all these kids going around west London proudly wearing QPR gear, not Chelsea or Fulham?"

Now, with the January transfer window just around the corner, Marsh acknowledges, "I wouldn't buy any fading Premiership stars in the transfer window. I think that sends out the wrong message. If I was at QPR now, I'd be looking for the next 21-year-old Rodney Marsh. It sounds arrogant I know, but it's not meant to be, because when you buy someone they should be for the next five or 10 years.

"When I joined QPR in my early twenties, I was at the top of my game at Fulham. Alec Stock recognised I could play, so I think QPR should be going after another young star of tomorrow. In fact, I would take it a step forward, and this would be the second part of my philosophy for QPR.

"If I was chief executive of QPR, I would sign a manager to a five-year contract. I would go out and research around the world for the best young manager for the job. And when I'd identified him, I would do my utmost to get him. I'd be looking for the next Arsene Wenger, he's out there somewhere, and I would make a commitment to him of a five-year contract, so that he could forge the way QPR would play on the pitch. My research would have drawn up a list of five possible managers from around the world, aged about 40.

"From what I can see, they've struggled to find the right manager so far. Paulo Sousa is their fifth appointment in two years, including caretaker managers, isn't he? You see, I don't think QPR should be rushing to be successful. They should be making sure that all the preparations are in place. It's not vital that they go up this season. But what is very important is that they make the play-offs.

"It's very important for the fans to see that progress is being made, which takes me back to my earlier point about getting the balance between what's right for the customers, the fans and the product, the team.

"The fans will want to enjoy the drama of the play-offs and see QPR competing there – but, in all honesty, probably the best thing would be for QPR to not be victorious in the play-offs, and to come back stronger next year when they'd be competing for automatic promotion and could really take the Championship by storm.

"This season so far, I wouldn't say QPR are in the top four sides in the Championship. And time and time again, you see sides set unrealistic targets, going up to the Premiership when they had absolutely no chance of staying up. The worst thing that could happen would be that you end up like West Brom this year, fighting every week to stay up.

"I don't think you need to spend lots of money to be promoted. But I think a successful side needs what I call a franchise player if it wants to stay in the Premiership. A Steven Gerrard, a David Beckham or a Rodney Marsh or Stan Bowles, a player that the fans are going to love and who will do it for you week in, week out. QPR don't have one of those players right now, and Briatore will need a player like this if he wants to kick on to the next level with the club."

Government minister and lifelong QPR fan Alan Johnson – MP for Kingston Upon Hull West and Hessle – says that the way money drives success in football makes him feel distinctly uncomfortable:

"I don't like it, I don't feel right with it, but neither do Chelsea fans, I'm sure. But it's the way football is going – or has gone. I'm an MP in Hull, and I hope rugby league doesn't go the same way. They are really trying to get Hull's kids through into the Hull rugby league team. But that's not happening with football, it seems.

"I don't think any true football fan likes this. But once you're in that world and you haven't got that kind of money coming into the club, if you haven't got a few entrepreneurs behind you, you might find it hard to compete.

"Interestingly, I met Briatore at halftime when QPR went up to play Hull last season. And I said to him, 'You're not thinking of moving away from Loftus Road, are you?' He replied, 'Why would I want to move away from Loftus Road? It is only 10 minutes from Harrods . . .' Johnson laughs out loud, adding, '10 minutes by Formula One car maybe . . .'"

Having seen Hull City promoted to the Premiership last season, Johnson wonders why QPR are struggling so far. "Maybe their mind's been on being one of the favourites, everyone saying they're going to be a Premier League club, and this is a horrible division to get out of.

"Look at Hull City last year. They had to fight and scrap and all the rest of it. I don't want to see QPR become another Stoke

City or whatever, but we need to think, 'How do we get out of this division?' We need to make and score goals, but we need the ability to win this division and plan for how we're going to stay in the Premiership.

"I think I did say in a magazine article once that I would like to be QPR manager, but actually Paulo Sousa's got the worst job of the lot. Overseeing QPR's travel arrangements or their publicity would be better for me. You don't have the pressure!"

Football is now an intense, high-stakes, multimillion-pound industry. "I don't know what you can do about the financial side of the football business. Maybe the credit crunch will lead to a similar problem in football to what they've had in the financial services – a kind of 'back to basics'. But it's considered to be good entertainment. Television rights are very important.

"It's much more of a financial game now and the club doesn't feel part of the community in the way that it did before. I know what will happen, they'll end up in the Premiership and no one will be able to get in unless they've got a season ticket. You won't be able to do what I do with my son, just pop down to the stadium, find somewhere to park and get in.

"That won't happen unless you can buy a season ticket, which a lot of people can't afford. They'll feel frozen out, which will be a real shame. Because QPR, the only club I know intimately in London terms, is much more a community village club than any other in the capital.

"Andy Burnham [Secretary for Sport at the time of the interview] talks some good sense about there being a need for a quota system. I'm quite keen on the quota, bringing young kids through. There's that famous fact about the Celtic team, isn't there? When they won the European Cup in 1967, the whole team was born within 30 miles of Parkhead.

"And look at the great QPR side of the mid-70's. Yes, we

bought Stan Bowles for a record fee at the time and then we paid a lot of money for Dave Thomas, but we also had local boys like Ian Gillard, Dave Clement and Gerry Francis, they came through the system at the club."

While the new owners have brought fresh hope, there are plenty of unanswered questions about what lies ahead. "It took us so long to battle out of the old third division and get up into the top flight, and it's taken us much longer than anyone thought to get back up there again.

"I'm spoilt by the fact that we were the top London side in the Premiership, that team of Les Ferdinand and Trevor Sinclair. And I thought we'd be back there much quicker than it's turning out."

Alan Johnson fears that QPR will end up being a mid-table Championship team again this season. "The other point to bear in mind is that it's alright having lots of money, but not everyone wants to play for a side in the Championship. Those days are gone. You could get Rodney Marsh to play in the third division back then, or Stan Bowles in the second, but players don't do that anymore. So you could have all the money in the world and not sign the great players."

But seeing Hull force their way into the play-offs last season also offers hope. "Hull was much further down the table than QPR at this stage of the season and they came late in a great surge. The whole of the city of Hull got caught up in it because they'd never been in the top flight. And Hull didn't have QPR's money, nowhere near it.

"The players were mostly journeymen. Even the Brazilian Geovanni was perceived as a has-been and was picked up on a free transfer. What you did see in this Hull success was the same atmosphere that surrounded the Rodney team of the 60's that won the League Cup and entered the top division for the first time, because Hull hadn't been in the top division either."

Composer and QPR fanatic Michael Nyman wonders if the club is already too far adrift from the top runners in the Championship. "We're obviously behind the likes of Wolves and Birmingham, who are the favourites to get automatic promotion.

"And while I didn't really know Paulo Sousa as a player, that doesn't mean he wasn't a good one who loved to play attractive football. They all seem to respect Sousa at QPR, but I can't see it happening this season. And if we did get promotion this season, I don't know how many players from the current team are Premiership players.

"We should be buying Premiership quality, so that if we get promotion we'll have players of that level already in the squad. If we got promotion and then bought a new team, that would not be good for the club or the fans, because we wouldn't have any sense of continuity.

"The January transfer window is important. We've got a new head coach and it will be interesting to see what happens. With the credit crunch there may not be many players moving to Premiership clubs, so there could be movement in our direction.

"And if there aren't any purchases then it's just tinkering, which doesn't seem to be showing a serious intent.

"I remember seeing Stan Bowles playing for Carlisle against QPR. We had the ability to see a player of his quality, then pick up the player and sign him from under the noses of richer clubs."

Nyman hopes that Rangers hasn't gone into total reverse. "We are one of the richest teams in the world now and could buy any player we want . . . but we don't."

CHAPTER TEN

STAN BOWLES HAD joined QPR in September 1972, for a then-record club fee of £112,000. It was 20 years later that composer Michael Nyman created a piece of music that was effectively a homage to the most popular player in the history of the club, the iconic wearer of the famous Number 10 shirt.

Entitled 'The Final Score', its showcase was a short film of the same title screened on Channel Four in 1992, at the height of the period when football became trendy in media circles. (Nick Hornby's landmark book about football obsession, *Fever Pitch*, was published in the same year.)

Nyman's instrumental music was set to images of Stan Bowles from the final match of the 1975-76 season, against Leeds United. Rangers had won 2-0 and finished second in the country's top division, their highest-ever league position.

"I was researching the film on a tour bus in Spain," says Nyman. "Everyone thought I was watching porn, but I was watching the much higher porn of 70's football. I was watching ITV's *The Big Match* or BBC's *Match of the Day*. It ended up being a love letter to Stan, but was not intended to be at the start. But that's the clips that were chosen, and that's how they panned out."

The film shows Dave Thomas scoring the first goal against

Leeds with a header, then Bowles scores the second in the 82nd minute, his 10th goal of the season, another sublime piece of skill. Frank McLintock picks him out with a pass of pinpoint precision; Bowles collects the ball, cuts inside and drives left-footed into the corner beyond David Harvey in the Leeds goal. The victory takes place in front of 31,002 fans, still a record attendance at Loftus Road.

But the film also includes newspaper cuttings revealing Stan's infamous tabloid exploits. Both sides of Bowles are presented: the maverick on the pitch – and the maverick off it too. Wearing the iconic shirt vacated by Marsh held no anxieties for Bowles.

"I hadn't heard of Rodney Marsh to tell the truth," he confesses. "I had absolutely no problem with wearing the Number 10 shirt that used to be his, it was no big deal to me."

Bowles grew up on the tough streets of Manchester. He played for Manchester City, Crewe and Carlisle before he was signed by QPR manager Gordon Jago, the club having finished the previous season fourth in the old Division Two.

These were the days before promotion play-offs, so Jago wanted to build a team that could force its way into the top two positions this time around, but with a nucleus of exciting young players who could also hold their own when promoted to the top flight. A comparison with QPR's current situation is striking: a team in football's second tier, trying to gain entry to the first, while building up a side to compete at the higher level.

Using the £200,000 from the sale of Rodney Marsh, Jago bought Bowles for a club record, then broke it again a month later to buy Dave Thomas from Burnley for £165,000. In addition, he acquired Don Givens from Luton Town, for £40,000. He already had Gerry Francis, Dave Clement and Ian Gillard coming up through the ranks, and had signed goalkeeper Phil Parkes from Walsall in 1970 – all future England internationals. Add to these young talents the experienced head of Terry Venables, who marshalled the midfield, and promotion was assured.

"Gordon was the instigator of the overall plan," explains Bowles. "He was the manager. But Terry Venables was still there then, and he used to do a lot of the coaching. Gordon had the ideas. I liked Gordon, but he didn't like me. Every time I got into trouble, he used to get this big red eye, it was like a twitch," he laughs.

"But when QPR went up to the First Division, as it was then, you could see it was a club with ambition." One man was the driving force behind the club's ascent to the highest echelons of English football: chairman Jim Gregory.

"Jim was putting a bit of money about, and he built that club with his own money. He wanted it to be successful. But he was no fool. You wouldn't get everything you wanted. You've got to remember, he was a second-hand car dealer, know what I mean? . . . In his Crombie coat he was a bit like George Cole from *Minder*, but without the coward bit.

"When we got into the First Division, we just clicked as a team. And at the start of the 1975-76 season we beat Liverpool at home, who came second the previous season, and two games later we beat Derby away at the Baseball Ground, the reigning champions. It was clear we had a good team that could do well at this level."

In October 1974, Gordon Jago resigned as QPR boss after falling out with chairman Gregory and joined Tampa Bay Rowdies in the United States, where he would join up with Rodney Marsh, already playing for the North American Soccer League club in Florida.

He was replaced by Dave Sexton, who had masterminded Chelsea's victories in the FA Cup and European Cup Winners' Cup. "I never liked Dave Sexton at first," says Bowles. "I thought he had some strange ideas and I had some major arguments with him.

"Sometimes he had us training and we didn't even have a ball. But I came round to his way of thinking. He used to go abroad to study coaching methods. He learnt about motivation techniques as well, and used to say things like, 'When the going gets tough, the tough get going.' I thought, 'Don't worry about me – I'm from Manchester.'

"On the pitch, me and Gerry Francis just clicked straight away. I thought, 'You'll do for me,' and that was the start of the partnership. And Dave Thomas worked with us as well. He was very important because he was so quick."

Bowles had a special bond with the Rangers fans. He used to go for a drink with them in the Springbok pub in South Africa Road, near the ground. "Back in Manchester that was the done thing, you went for a drink with the fans all the time.

"When I came to London, I found out it wasn't like that here. I said, 'It is for me,' so I used to go into the Springbok against Dave Sexton's expressed wishes, because Rangers players were barred from having a drink in a pub within two miles of the ground. The Springbok was about 200 yards away.

"I used to pop in there after a game and I still go there now. Back then, I'd be there after every home game more or less. I went wherever I wanted to go. Before the games, I used to sometimes arrive in the dressing-room at about 2.45 and Dave would be asking 'Where's Stan, where's Stan?'

"Don Shanks used to cover up for me because I was in the betting shop. They wanted to put up a statue in Belfast for George Best, didn't they? Well, I said if they should ever put one up for me, it should be outside the betting shop in South Africa Road.

"Fans used to shout out racing results to me from the crowd during the game. You know how close the crowd is to the players at Loftus Road – they can touch you. And I used to just lark about with them. When I was on form, I could do anything.

"Opposing players and fans thought I was arrogant, and they didn't like me because I used to take the piss. We were by far the most entertaining team in the country that season. When we had a midweek game we'd have 10 or 15 managers sitting in the stand watching us. George Graham told me that.

"That 1975-76 team is obviously the most successful side I played in. If I popped the ball 20 yards in front of Dave Thomas on the wing, I knew he'd get it. He was that quick. But then if I made a mistake with the pass, I'd put my hands up in frustration and make out to the fans it was his fault. And the fans would have a go at him." Bowles laughs as he remembers the cheekiness of it all. "I could do no wrong in the eyes of the fans and I loved all that, but I did abuse it."

If he's forced to compare the side of today to that of his era, in his opinion there's only one winner. "I don't know about the QPR side now, but I think we had a bit more talent back then. Obviously we didn't bring in foreign players and we had local kids coming through."

Indeed, Gerry Francis was born in Chiswick and fullback Ian Gillard in Hammersmith, both just down the road from Loftus Road. "But kids can't come through now like they did then," says Bowles. "And I said this a few years ago, because they buy these foreign players.

"The club is still in with a chance of the play-offs, of course, and, with the money they've got behind them, they will go up eventually. They can buy success on the pitch, and the players now are fitter.

"But we had some good players back then. And the highlight for me didn't come in that 1975-76 season. It was the following year, when I broke the scoring record in Europe of Denis Law. That was my favourite memory." Bowles set a single-season record at the time of 11 goals in Europe during QPR's UEFA Cup run, reaching the quarter-final stage before being knocked out by AEK Athens on penalties.

"I found it easy playing in Europe. In fact, I nearly joined the German club Hamburg in the summer before that 1976-77 season began, and that was before Kevin Keegan had joined them as well. But I don't like Germans.

"I was supposed to meet them in a hotel and the chairman, Jim Gregory, didn't turn up, so I went into the foyer to ring him up. He said he wasn't coming and, if I wanted, I could jump in a taxi and leave too. Go round to his place in the morning, he said, and we'd talk about a new contract. So I did.

"You know what Germans are like. There must have been about 15 of them. And I left them there. Then Kevin Keegan joins Hamburg a year later and is European Footballer of the Year! Personally, I don't think I could play under a foreign coach. When they start ranting and raving in their own language . . . "

Like Rodney Marsh before him, Bowles had a special relationship with Gregory, who obviously liked to look after his star players. "It was common knowledge that Jim was giving me £200 on a Monday morning," says Bowles. "And Don Masson heard about this.

"Now he was a blinding player, but I didn't think much of him as a person, do you know what I mean? And he goes to Jim, 'How come I'm not getting £200 as well?' and Jim says, 'You're not as good as Bowlesey, so you're getting nothing.'

"Jim was the best chairman I ever played for and I gave him one of my England caps. He's dead now, of course, but I assume one of his family has got it."

Off the pitch, Bowles was becoming notorious for headline-grabbing exploits. Gambling debts were mounting as he searched for ways to make a few extra quid. On one occasion, he was photographed with a topless model for the front page of *The*

Daily Mirror. He was paid £500, but soon regretted the photo session ever taking place. Ann, his wife at the time, left him and moved back to Manchester.

The press tried to make out that Bowles and the model were having an affair, but he'd only met her once. The situation was also stressing out the model and her boyfriend. She was later involved in a car accident that put her in a coma for a while and ruined her career.

The reporters were constantly on his tail, hunting for a story, so Bowles tried to outmanoeuvre them. "I was telling them, 'Write what you want, I don't care.' One time I did a story in the press that I'd retired on a Friday, but then I was back in training on the Monday. That reporter never spoke to me for years afterwards, funnily enough.

"I had loads of gambling problems and they were with gangsters, so you had to pay and that was a worry. But once I went onto the pitch, it took me away from my problems. It was a release. Nothing fazed me on a football pitch. I was confident in my own ability as a player."

One young QPR fan was captivated by Bowles as he dominated the stage at Loftus Road. Ron Lewis, now a boxing writer on *The Times*, has been a season-ticket holder at Loftus Road for 34 years. His first season ticket was for the 1975-76 season, when he was just six years old.

"Stan Bowles was my hero," he says. "He was clearly a very inspirational player. At the time I was watching him, I didn't look at *The Sun* or anything. Whatever was in the tabloids about him was by the by and meant nothing to me. I used to just read about him in the programme, or in *Shoot* magazine or *Roy of the Rovers*."

Adds Lewis, "I can always remember where my first season ticket was back then – Block R, Row H, Seat 8 in the Ellerslie Road stand, and it was right in line with the goal-line. Stan used to come over and take the corner kicks in front of me, right in front of the Loft. I could see the swerve he used to put on the ball and everything. I had a perfect view from my seat. Stan was just the ultimate hero and still is.

"In my job now as a journalist, I meet loads of famous people, it's just part of the job, and they just become another famous person. But there are a few people who I know I would struggle to talk to if I met them, because they are my heroes. I've been in rooms with Stan Bowles in the past, but I've always declined to speak to him because he falls into that category."

To a young lad, Bowles oozed cool. "There was a game against Middlesbrough once when he got the ball in the corner, turned around and hit this shot with the outside of his foot. He didn't hit it very hard, but he scored with a curved banana kick.

"It's interesting because we look back at that era today and we revel in his tabloid image, but he was a hero of mine and that image had nothing to do with it at all. I never read the *News of the World*, *The Sun* or *The Mirror* at the time, so I had no idea about these tabloid stories.

"His existence to me was purely on a football pitch. As a kid you'd hear vague stories about his gambling and the classic story that he'd supposedly go to the betting shop in South Africa Road to put a bet on the 2.45 race or whatever, but I think that made him more of a story as we look back with nostalgia.

"It's not necessarily true about what made him popular for Rangers fans at the time. What made him popular was that he was the totem pole that this fantastic team was built around. Every Rangers fan remembers every member of that team and Stan was the greatest."

When QPR beat Leeds United in the last home game of the 1975-76 season – the subject of Michael Nyman's film – they were top of the league. But, because of European commitments, they had to wait 10 days until their nearest rivals, Liverpool, played their final match against Wolverhampton Wanderers.

If Liverpool won they would be champions, but if they lost, it would be QPR. "I remember where I was the day we lost the title that season. I was at a Gilbert and Sullivan show in St Mary's Church Hall in Hanwell," says Lewis. "We knew people who were in it and I remember at the interval being told that Liverpool were one down, which meant we were champions. But by the final curtain, Wolves had lost 1-3."

Wolves held onto their 1-0 lead until 13 minutes from time, when Kevin Keegan equalised for Liverpool. John Toshack and Ray Kennedy scored two more before the end to ensure the title went to Anfield. QPR was less than a quarter of an hour from being crowned the best team in the land. Liverpool won the league by one point.

"It was just the absolute outrage that Liverpool could play that game 10 days after we'd played our last game of the season against Leeds. They knew the score and could throw everything at it because they knew they had to win.

"Whereas if we'd been playing at the same time it could have been a bit different, the advantage can change hands in a moment. They might have thought a draw would have been sufficient and then end up losing the title if we stole a late winner. That situation would never have been allowed to happen today, it was so unfair on Rangers.

"All through school I was usually the only QPR fan in the class, especially when I went to Westminster City, a comprehensive secondary school near Victoria. Most of the other kids were Liverpool fans, and the huge irony of this was that, by the time I was aged about 13, my brother was at university up north, and I started to regularly go to away games with him.

"I'd actually see Liverpool play more than any of these kids would. These kids were Liverpool fans by seeing them on *Match of the Day* and by buying a shirt in a local sports store. I would see Liverpool at least once, often twice a season. They would never have been to Anfield but they would say, 'We beat you . . .' It really irritated me."

By the 2008-09 season, Bowles was no longer a regular face at Loftus Road anymore, though the club – and especially the fans – were clearly still in his heart. "I don't really know the new owners now. The only dealing I've had with them is that they said I may get some work at the club, but it hasn't happened. It was a bit confusing at the time. But I'm not bothered. I'm fine. I rarely go to see Rangers now. The last game was the first game of this season, that's it."

Adds Bowles, "My bond is with the fans. They like me and I like them. I go for a drink with them, and I know lots of Rangers fans who've named their boys Stanley. I know seven who've done that, I think, there's probably more. And that's quite a compliment. But there's no doubt that, with the money behind the club now, they could and should become successful again.

"QPR made me. And QPR fans are the ones I'm closest to. They're the most passionate that I know. QPR is all about tradition and dads passing their support of the club down to their sons. I've seen it. I've lived around west London now for 30-odd years.

"I remember on one occasion last season, this big shaven-headed bloke was walking outside Loftus Road with his boy. He points at me and says to him, 'That's the best player QPR has ever had.' And his son replies, 'But I've never heard of him, Dad . . .' That made me laugh and it just sums it up for me."

This one comment by a young boy reveals so much. QPR was a side with a great history, but in desperate need of fresh success. Young fans had been starved of genuine heroes like Stan Bowles and Rodney Marsh.

But would that change under the new regime at the club? Would a new icon emerge in the famous Number 10 shirt? Were the glory days about to return?

And was Paulo Sousa the man to bring them back?

CHAPTER ELEVEN

WHEN PAULO SOUSA was unveiled as QPR's new first team coach in November 2008, one of the team's star players was already fully aware of the Portuguese's immense importance to a winning team – something he'd known since they first 'worked' together 10 years earlier.

Lee Cook explains: "When I was about 17 or 18, a computer game called Championship Manager was all the rage, and I used to sign Paulo Sousa because he was a vital player in a winning formation for that game: 4-1-3-2. To win, you always needed to have a good defensive midfielder, someone sitting in front of the back four. He used to do a great job for me in the game. I knew he was a top player."

Championship Manager was launched in 1992, later evolving into Football Manager and becoming a phenomenal success. In it you pretended to be a football boss, buying and selling players and winning trophies. The game became a cult hit with a generation of young fans, teaching them about players from different countries around the world.

In today's real game, an in-depth knowledge of world football is also essential for a manager or coach. So there was an air of optimism around Sousa's arrival at Loftus Road, armed (or at least the fans hoped) with an impressive black book of football contacts.

Ron Lewis, a QPR season ticket holder for 34 years, had seen plenty of managers come and go but was positive about the future under the new boss: "One of the advantages for Sousa is that he comes from outside the club and Championship football, giving it a fresh perspective. Luigi De Canio came from outside as well and, while it wasn't a very successful campaign last season, we did play some nice football at times, and how much more entertaining was that than what we've been seeing this season under Dowie?

"I'm confident that Sousa won't settle for any rubbish. You can imagine that, after the career he's had as a player, he's got high standards and that most of the players look up to him because of what he's achieved. You also imagine that he's got his own ideas and that he's not afraid to try players out."

Sousa's results after taking control at the end of November were impressive. Before the end of 2008, there were victories at home over Charlton and high-flying Wolves, the latter in front of the Sky Sports cameras. There were also draws away against Crystal Palace and Plymouth, with just one defeat away to Sheffield Wednesday sandwiched in between.

The victory over top-of-the-table Wolves, which brought the visitors' eight-match unbeaten run to an end, saw one of the goals of the season at Loftus Road – as captain Martin Rowlands won the game with a stunning 25-yard strike.

After the Wolves victory, striker Patrick Agyemang told reporters that Sousa had made an immediate difference: "He's very strict in training. He wants it done his way and he wants you to listen to him all the time. He's always drumming things into our heads. He's playing with this diamond formation which he wants everyone to know. We're having meetings every day, watching videos

"Sometimes it is like going back to school, but it's good. It's all part of a footballer's job. If we're at training longer than we're supposed to be, so be it. As long as we get the three points, it's okay."

Sousa was making his mark on all the players. As Lee Cook says, "He was recognised as a good, up-and-coming young manager working with Portugal, and it was never going to be easy for him coming over to the Championship in this country, but he started really well.

"Training was completely different to how it was under Iain Dowie. Straightaway he worked on our positional sense, where we should be at certain moments in a game. In the first few games we were doing what he was saying and it was working. If we were winning, he would change the formation to see a game out, and if we were losing he would change the formation then as well, to try to win the game. Probably the best example of that was when we beat Preston at home."

When Preston North End visited Loftus Road in December they were occupying the final play-off position with six more points than QPR, who were ninth. To harbour any realistic play-off ambitions at the end of the season, this was the sort of game QPR had to win. But, after Preston was awarded a dubious penalty in the second half, the score was 2-2.

Three points were slipping away when Sousa made a bold double substitution with 10 minutes to go. Two fullbacks, Peter Ramage and Damien Delaney, were taken off and replaced by one central defender, Fitz Hall, and one striker, Dexter Blackstock. Rangers switched from 4-4-2 to an attacking 3-4-3 formation that swung the game Sousa's way.

Substitute Blackstock made an impact almost straightaway. With four minutes to go, Cook was fouled on the left. Martin Rowlands curled in the resulting free-kick to find Blackstock towering over the opposing defence to score a superb header in the top corner and make it 3-2.

Sousa leapt off the bench as the players celebrated in front of the Loft. QPR's strong home form since the Portuguese had taken over had brought a play-off position firmly within reach.

The Preston game was also considered by many fans to be Lee Cook's best performance since returning to QPR in the summer. He'd run the opposition ragged. Three days later he got busy on his website blog: "I absolutely love playing in the new system under Paulo Sousa at QPR. He called me into the office on the first day that he was here and talked me through what he expected of me and how important he thought I would be to the team. Coming from someone like him that means a lot.

"He was a player I watched when he was at Inter and for Portugal. He was my kind of footballer, a skilful ball player. Even now, when he gets involved in training you can see he's still got the touch, the geezer oozes class."

Cook enjoyed playing in the diamond formation favoured by Sousa: "He's given me a lot of confidence and I'm relishing the chance to play at the tip of the diamond. It's a position I used to play in when I was 17 or 18 years old so it's not a strange role for me. I think it really suits me and hopefully I can make that spot my own.

"There's plenty of competition at the minute though. If you looked at the bench for last Saturday's game, we had Fitz Hall, Mikele Leigertwood, Dexter Blackstock, Emmanuel Ledesma and Samuel Di Carmine all ready to come on.

"That's a lot of quality to have in reserve, and Dex came on and got the winner against Preston just to show that. Everyone's fighting for their place and that's what you need if you're going to challenge for promotion."

Fans hoped they could build on this success a week later, by beating Charlton – then threatened with relegation – away on Boxing Day and muscling into the play-off positions. But instead of sticking with the winning side which had impressed against Preston, Sousa made six changes to the starting line-up. A game QPR should have won ended in a 2-2 draw. Sousa's tinkering was blamed for the lost points.

More changes to personnel were on the cards when the January transfer window opened the following week. But there were already lots of comings and goings within the squad. The loan spell of Spanish Under-21 midfielder Daniel Parejo came to an end in mid-December, after Real Madrid recalled him to help with an injury crisis at the Bernabeu.

The 19-year-old had agreed a one-year loan with Rangers in the summer, but Madrid activated a clause to bring him back to Spain. The player had arrived at the club with a glowing reputation, but came under fire from some sections of the crowd who believed he failed to live up to expectations.

Another foreign player leaving the club was the former Roma star and Italian international Damiano Tommasi, who would always be remembered at Loftus Road for his man-of-the-match performance when QPR beat Birmingham City in the snow, during Gareth Ainsworth's period in charge. His one-year contract, which had been signed in September, was terminated in January by mutual consent.

And the foreign player who made the most impact during his short stay at Loftus Road was also leaving. Argentine Emmanuel Ledesma, 20, who joined QPR on a one-year loan from Italian Serie A side Genoa, returned to Italy to join Serie B side Salernitana on loan instead. His deal with QPR was terminated by mutual consent at the start of February.

Ledesma had made 23 appearances in all competitions and scored four goals, the highlight being a 29-minute hat-trick against Carlisle in the second round of the Carling Cup back in August. It was rumoured on message boards that a fee was in place to buy him if the loan spell was a success, but he struggled to repeat his early-season form.

There may have been a clearout of some Latin stars, but those from colder climes were travelling in the opposite direction. Icelandic striker Heidar Helguson signed a loan deal in November, with a view to a permanent move from Premiership side Bolton if he could prove his form and fitness.

All was now set for the transfer window to open on January 1. Would QPR snap up a star player who might enable them to make the play-offs? Would the rich owners flash the cash? In the end, five players signed on the dotted line – either permanently or on loan – and two left the club.

Gary Borrowdale joined from Coventry (for an undisclosed fee), Heidar Helguson's loan deal was turned into a permanent transfer (undisclosed), Wayne Routledge signed from Aston Villa (undisclosed), Lee Cook became a full-fledged Rangers player again and not a loan signing from Fulham anymore (undisclosed) and Liam Miller moved to QPR from Sunderland on loan (undisclosed). Moving out of Loftus Road, Zesh Rehman joined Bradford City on loan and Adam Bolder moved to Millwall on a free.

While Gary Borrowdale failed to make an appearance for the first team, Wayne Routledge and Liam Miller both looked interesting signings. But were they enough to secure promotion?

Winger Routledge joined QPR from Aston Villa, despite a late effort by Cardiff City to make a loan deal with them permanent. He had joined Aston Villa from Spurs for £1,250,000 in August 2008, but made only two starts and appeared as a substitute only six times. He wasn't able to push his way past England internationals Ashley Young or James Milner into the first team.

Irish international Miller joined Rangers on loan until the end of the season, when a permanent move would be explored if he impressed at Loftus Road. It was believed that the Republic of Ireland manager, the legendary Giovanni Trapattoni, brought Miller to the attention of the Rangers board, leading to his loan deal.

Miller began his career at Celtic before joining Manchester United in 2004, moving to Sunderland in 2006 where he made 60 appearances, scoring three goals. As Miller said at the time, "The manager has great ideas about where he wants to take us. The play-offs are our aim and there's no reason why we can't achieve our objectives."

QPR were bubbling away just outside the play-offs, so there was a sense of optimism going into the January fixtures. But Rangers would have to compete through early 2009 without three stalwarts of the side. Akos Buzsaky, regarded by most fans as the club's most talented footballer, had already missed the opening six weeks of the campaign due to an ankle operation. But more woe was to come the way of the Hungarian international.

He damaged the anterior cruciate ligament in his knee during the defeat to Manchester United in the Carling Cup in November, and was out for the rest of the season. Meanwhile, Rowan Vine, another of the squad's most skilful players, was still struggling to recover from a serious broken leg he'd suffered the previous April, which had kept him out for the whole season so far.

Then, in January, captain Martin Rowlands was added to the injury list when he was carried off against Derby after only 12 minutes at Pride Park, with another anterior cruciate ligament knee injury. He would also be out for the rest of the season. To lift their spirits, fans hoped for impressive performances from new recruits during the January transfer window, and Wayne Routledge for one did not disappoint.

The game at Pride Park was supposed to celebrate the appointment of Nigel Clough as Derby manager, joining the club that his father Brian had led to the old First Division title. Clough senior had taken Derby from the Second Division to become champions of England and European Cup semi-finalists during his spell in charge, from June 1967 to October 1973. But this game was going to be a harsh introduction to the hot-seat for his 42-year-old son.

Routledge was rampant, in just his second game for QPR. He scored in the 22nd minute, then turned provider for Mikele Leigertwood, who tucked away the second goal in the 36th minute for an impressive 0-2 victory away from home.

Just as losing 0-2 to Derby at Loftus Road in September had signalled the start of Iain Dowie's downfall, perhaps this reversal of the scoreline at Pride Park might herald the rise of Sousa. Only time would tell.

Three days later, Rangers beat Blackpool 0-3 away. This had also proven a tricky home fixture for Dowie three months earlier, which QPR could only draw 1-1. But Rangers were now hitting a rich form, and fans could only imagine how good this side would be if Akos Buzsaky, Rowan Vine and Martin Rowlands were also available.

As season-ticket holder Ron Lewis said: "Looking at the team at the moment, we're all waiting for the return of Vine and Buzsaky from injury. The system that Sousa likes to play with the diamond formation in midfield seems ideal for Buzsaky, I think he's our most gifted player. He could play at the front of it.

"Routledge looks a good player. You want threatening players and he's obviously that. Potentially, if we've got Cook and Routledge on either wing performing well, we look a really threatening team."

But the player who caught the fan's eye the most was not in attack. "This season, I think the best player has been Damion Stewart in defence. He was a player that had been written off as hopeless in the past. People have had faith in him this year and he wasn't even in the team at the start of the season.

"It just shows that if you give a guy with talent some time, and you show some faith in him, he can come good. There is this mentality at the moment among Rangers fans that if you go out there and have a bad game, then we should sell you. Fans want us to win every game and that's just not realistic. We're not Chelsea, we're not Manchester United.

"Sousa has the brain to know we're not going to win every game. I don't want us to go up this year anyway. If we went up, we could turn into a kind of Fulham, buying a load of Premiership cast-off players at inflated wages. I hope that next year we go up, and we build a squad under Sousa that plays well.

"Then we don't have to scrape around for a Jimmy Bullard or an Emile Heskey, or a Darren or Marcus Bent, a player who's been around the houses. We would have our own core of talented players who would hopefully step up to Premiership level. That would be ideal."

At the end of January, second-placed Reading visited Loftus Road for a game that finished 0-0. This time it was the turn of midfielder Liam Miller to catch the eye, another purchase in the January window, now making his home debut. Like Wolves and Birmingham City before them, Reading could not score against QPR at Loftus Road.

The so-called 'Big Three' in the Championship failed to break down a Rangers defence that looked stronger and stronger as the season progressed. Alongside Damion Stewart at the heart of it, Latvian Kaspars Gorkss was proving a shrewd buy from Blackpool in the summer. With goalkeeper Radek Cerny and defender Matthew Connolly also impressing, QPR was solid at the back.

Paulo Sousa's side was entering the final third of the season just outside the play-off positions, in seventh place. Fans were looking forward to what the rest of the season would bring. Wayne Routledge and Liam Miller looked like useful additions to the squad and, while Martin Rowlands and Akos Buzsaky would be missing due to injury for the remains of the season, a position in the play-offs still looked like a genuine possibility.

Very quickly, however, the atmosphere would turn nasty at Loftus Road. It would be nearly a month before the next home game, against Ipswich in front of the Sky Sports TV cameras – a game that everyone associated with QPR probably wishes to forget.

Then the expectations of fans would come under the spotlight as much as the players on the pitch and the first team coach in the dugout, as the season began to implode.

NOVEMBER/DECEMBER

PAULO SOUSA AS FIRST TEAM COACH

QPR 2-1 Charlton

25 November 2008
Attendance: 12,286
Scorers: Blackstock (2)
Table: 10th with 28 points

Crystal Palace 0-0 QPR

29 November 2008
Attendance: 16,411
Visiting Rangers fans: 1,579
Table: 9th with 29 points

QPR 1-0 Wolves
6 December 2008
Attendance: 13,416
Scorer: Rowlands
Table: 7th with 32 points

Sheffield Wednesday 1-0 QPR
9 December 2008
Attendance: 14,792
Visiting Rangers fans: 376
Table: 9th with 32 points

Plymouth Argyle 1-1 QPR
13 December 2008
Attendance: 10,747
Visiting Rangers fans: 657
Scorer: Helguson
Table: 9th with 33 points

QPR 3-2 Preston North End
20 December 2008
Attendance: 14,103
Scorers: Helguson (2), Blackstock
Table: 9th with 36 points

Charlton 2-2 QPR
26 December 2008
Attendance: 21,023
Visiting Rangers fans: 2,323
Scorers: Blackstock, Cook
Table: 9th with 37 points

QPR 0-0 Watford
28 December 2008
Attendance: 16,196
Table: 9th with 38 points

JANUARY

PAULO SOUSA AS FIRST TEAM COACH

QPR 0-0 Burnley (FA Cup R3)
3 January 2009
Attendance: 8,896

QPR 1-1 Coventry
10 January 2009
Attendance: 13,330
Scorers: Blackstock
Table: 9th with 39 points

Burnley 2-1 QPR (FA Cup R3 replay, after extra time)
13 January 2009
Attendance: 3,760
Visiting Rangers fans: 288
Scorer: Di Carmine

Derby County 0-2 QPR
17 January 2009
Attendance: 28,390
Visiting Rangers fans: 1,082
Scorers: Routledge, Leigertwood
Table: 8th with 42 points

Blackpool 0-3 QPR

27 January 2009
Attendance: 6,656
Visiting Rangers fans: 315
Scorers: Helguson (2), Ephraim
Table: 7th with 45 points

QPR 0-0 Reading

31 January 2009
Attendance: 17,120
Table: 7th with 46 points

CHAPTER TWELVE

THE LATE 1980's had seen the birth of a football phenomenon that offered fans a voice they had never had before. Football fanzines sprang up in every corner of the league. Noisy, opinionated, irreverent and fearless, they shook up the game.

More than 20 years on, one of the country's very first football fanzines was still going strong. *A Kick up the R's* was launched in 1987, costing just 40p, in the wake of the failed attempt to merge QPR and Fulham into Fulham Park Rangers – a proposal that caused outrage among the fans of both west London clubs.

Other QPR fanzines came and went, including one called *All Quiet on the Western Avenue*, written by an aspiring rock musician and QPR fanatic named Pete Doherty. But *A Kick up the R's* is the only printed QPR fanzine still on the market.

In 2008 it was voted the best fanzine in the Championship. "The fanzine provides a terrific read for any football fan," praised the judges, who also acclaimed it for its design and overall presentation.

It was quite an accolade for the editor, Dave Thomas, who was always spotted selling the fanzine on match-days outside the stadium. He had the same name as one of the heroes from the great QPR team of the mid-70's that so nearly won the league, but his personal story was very different to that of most fans who grew up with strong family links to west London.

"I was born and raised on the Isle of Wight and we played football morning, noon and night," he says. "It was the 1966 World Cup that really fired our imaginations, which was also the year that my dad took me to my first game, which was Portsmouth v Hull in a cup replay.

"Southampton were playing Barrow in another replay as well, and I was excited all day because I didn't know which game we were going to, which turned out to be the Portsmouth game. Lots of kids end up supporting the first team they go and see, or indeed the opposition of the first team they go and see, but I stood out to be different and ended up supporting neither Portsmouth nor Hull.

"I was 11 in 1966 and it was the World Cup that inspired me to learn about grounds, clubs and players. We used to pore over tables and I remember seeing this club that was top of the third division, which to a kid was very impressive, and I suppose to a certain extent I was a bit of a glory hunter but I knew nothing about them. They didn't really have any relevance to me at the time.

"One of my abiding memories was at school. The school bully pushed me up against a wall in the playground and said, 'Who do you support, Thomas?' I can hear him saying it now, 42 years on, and it's a defining moment for me. The key question from the bully was, 'Do you support Portsmouth or Southampton?' Where I come from, everyone supports one or the other, it's the big divide. And I remember thinking, 'No, I support Queens Park Rangers.' And that was it.

"That's how it happened. I couldn't tell you the name of the kid or describe him, but I can picture myself in that playground. I think it was the very essence of wanting to be different to my mates. It takes a lot today for a kid not to support Chelsea or Manchester United, especially if they have older kids around them who support them, but I suppose that's effectively what I did back at that age.

"The odd thing is that I now feel some sort of moral superiority by being a QPR fan. If I'm outside Manchester and I see a car with Manchester United all over it, I snigger at them and I make sure they know I snigger at them, because I have this sense of moral superiority over them from being a QPR fan. Just like your credit card says a lot about you, so does the club you support. It's a statement."

After leaving school in 1973, Thomas went to sea and joined the Merchant Navy, which saw him away on voyage for nine months at a time – a period that coincided with the era of Stan Bowles and the other Dave Thomas, the star winger of the 1975-76 side that just missed out on winning the league.

"I backed QPR at 40-1," he says. "That's what the odds were, and I had a whole 50p on it, which back in the mid-70's was the equivalent of having a fiver now, and £20 winnings would have been a tidy sum. I don't know why I didn't bet the whole pound, but anyway . . .

"And I was following QPR from all points of the globe. I phoned my mate from America at about three in the morning one night to find out how we'd got on. Nowadays there's instant communication. But back then, with just shortwave radio, I missed the result at home to West Ham.

"So I rang up my mate and got him out of bed in the middle of the night to find out the score. I took time out from my job with the Merchant Navy to see the end of that 75-76 season – you're not supposed to do that. I bunked off effectively."

After 12 years living in London he moved to Shropshire and Crewe, before settling in Greater Manchester. But no matter where he lived in the UK, and despite the endless hours on the motorway, he would always be spotted at QPR games home and away.

"I'd say it's about a 450-mile round journey for each home game, which is a bit tedious when you come down midweek. But I love it. People say, 'How can you do that?' But to me travelling is part and parcel of the crack really. I think it would get very boring if it was just me, but it's not just me. There's an intricate network of people that we travel with.

"What people don't really understand is, when QPR play Burnley midweek away and there are 300 hardy souls, there's probably just one coach of fans. The other 240 who are not on the coach are probably made up of exiles. I'm not a born and bred Londoner, but there are also other people from other parts of the country who happen to support QPR for a million different reasons.

"We have a big Manchester R's contingent. It's a social network of QPR fans in Manchester. We have our annual barbecue and we have a QPR pub in the heart of Manchester that we've taken ownership of. In my position, you get to know that our support exceeds far outside west London.

"I got talking to a guy I see at games home and away and found out he lives in Lincoln. His routine is just as intricate as mine, but I only know about mine. When I sit next to you at a game, you don't know where I come from. You could be sitting next to someone from Leeds and they'll have a story too about why they do it.

"The guy I travel with, and who helps me with the fanzine, is Dave Anderson, who's born and bred in Burnley. Every time we go in for a meeting with the club the first thing that comes across the table is this thick Burnley accent, which we always have to get out of the way straightaway, explaining that he's really a QPR fan.

"Dave works for Jaguar now, so he lives in Coventry and we pick him up in Warwick. We pick up Malcolm in Stoke and we've got another lad, Denzil, who lives in Walsall. They're all season-ticket holders but we're not unique. At 9 o'clock on a Saturday morning, there are probably carloads setting off from all over the country to get to QPR. There are two lads from Blackpool who are season-ticket holders. You name any major city and I can probably name you fans from there."

It was the proposed merger with Fulham, in February 1987, which got Thomas actively involved in supporter issues for the first time. Jim Gregory, the chairman who had built QPR into a modern football club and overseen the eras of Rodney Marsh, in the 60's, and Stan Bowles, in the 70's, sold his controlling stake in the club for £5.5 million to Marler Estates, who already owned Fulham. Marler Estates was a property company, so there was a lot of speculation about why it would want to own two clubs in west London. Fans would find out soon enough.

Marler Estates proposed that QPR and Fulham should merge into one club called Fulham Park Rangers and play at Loftus Road, enabling them to turn Craven Cottage – a sought-after location overlooking the River Thames – into a luxury flats development called Boat Race Towers.

As Thomas remembers, "We all woke up one morning to the headline 'Fulham Park Rangers', and the stories that Fulham and Rangers were going to merge. By then I'd been a season-ticket holder at Rangers for a long time, but I'd never protested about anything. But this was different. It was my football club.

"I remember I was driving a lorry at the time and I scrawled on the back, 'QPR is dead, long live QPR.' A pretty pathetic thing to do, but all day long I was getting honks and thumbs up from people driving past in support, which I thought was quite bizarre.

"All QPR fans were waiting for something to happen. I read in the *Evening Standard* that there was going to be a meeting of Fulham and QPR fans in Vauxhall, south London. The Fulham guys were much more organised. They'd already had problems, threats that they were going to lose their ground, so they were organised because of that. It was pretty exciting to be involved, but at the end of the evening we hadn't really achieved anything."

Thomas found himself chatting at the bar with another protestor. "We realised we had to do something rather than sitting there just moaning about it, and between us we really took the initiative. Next morning, I went off sick to get some leaflets organised. On the Saturday, within 48 hours, we'd organised all these protests.

"We played Man City at home, a day etched on the memory. There was a pitch invasion and a sit-down protest on the pitch. And we were suddenly in demand. It was amazing. I'd never been involved in anything like this before. Never been interviewed, nothing like that, and suddenly I had newspapers ringing me up at midnight."

The moneymen behind the project completely underestimated the strength of public opinion. There was a remarkable display of solidarity by fans from all over London against the proposed merger, plus a stormy meeting on the subject organised by Hammersmith and Fulham Council. The issue was even raised in Parliament.

In the face of this intense protest the project was downgraded to a groundshare, and then dropped altogether when Marler Estates chairman David Bulstrode personally acquired QPR, bringing an end to talk of mergers and groundshares once and for all.

"On the Sunday and Monday after that Man City game, we

really took all the headlines. And, of course, the merger was called off. We actually went to meet David Bulstrode in a secret location, which turned out to be one of the houses in Loftus Road just down the road from the ground.

"But it was the sheer weight of protest against the merger that convinced him to take a step back and decide it wasn't going to happen. And the fanzine came out of that."

The campaign against the merger also led to the formation of an independent supporters' association for Rangers fans, one of the first of its kind in the country. It was Thomas's idea but he didn't get too involved in the mechanics of it, having the fanzine to concentrate on.

The influential football magazine *When Saturday Comes* – imbued with the same ethos as club fanzines – had also launched the previous year. The whole idea of fanzines was still very much in its infancy and only a few existed in the whole of the UK. "I remember we were trying to come up with a name, something wild and wacky. But maybe, 20 years down the line, the name is something I regret choosing.

"*A Kick up the R's* is now a brand name and everyone knows it, so I couldn't possibly change the title. But do I hate it today? Yeah, I hate it. I hate it because it doesn't sell it for me. We chose it at the time because *A Kick up the R's* was irreverent, out of leftfield, slightly subversive. Today, every now and again some bright spark says to us, 'That's just what they need,' like we haven't heard that a thousand times a season. Over 20 years, I've probably heard that a million times.

"If I was sitting down today to do a marketing plan to launch a new magazine, I would not call it that. But hey, 20 years ago that's what we called it and now it's too late to change it. But the fact is that it's the best fanzine in the country, bar none. Pound for pound, generally speaking, the stuff in there is incredible. I think it's also incredible that, 22 years down the line, it's still going strong. I was only going to do it for six months."

Despite his reservations about the name, Thomas believes *A Kick up the R's* has a significant role to play in the world of football. "I still think the fanzine is the voice of the conscience of the supporters. Its role is to reflect the mood and the climate among the fans.

"It's to reflect the culture of the club and to preserve its history and traditions, and to articulate the concerns of fans. But above everything else, it's to reinforce the values of what we are as a football club and what we are as supporters, what this football club means to every single individual.

"This is a club that makes people cry, it's that important. To many people it's one of the only constant threads through their lives, because relationships come and go. We love our football club like it's our family. That's not because we're all sad bastards with nothing else going on in our lives. I've got lots going on in my life. Is QPR the most important thing in my life? No. The people around me are the most important things in my life. But I cry for them too.

"To me, supporting QPR is about the people I know through the club, the emotions I experience. As daft as it may sound, QPR represents all the good things in life which we share. You fall out, have your ups and downs, you get the hump. But everything comes back to the core values. The respect you have for the people around you.

"I'm not being a scientist, stepping back and overanalysing it, but QPR defines me really. It defines me in a way that a lot of people may not understand. Not because I've got nothing else in my life, but because it's my way of expressing myself.

"I can't think of any other hobby or interest that can take you through the same gamut of emotions. It can happen in the space of 10 seconds. You can be down on the floor and then up in the air, and you can share these moments with complete strangers."

The situation that *A Kick up the R's* is now commenting on in 2009 is very different to the one it faced back in 1987. There are no concerns about a merger now, but much analysis of the impact of the current owners.

When the February edition of *FourFourTwo* football magazine carried the Football Rich List 2009, all three of QPR's co-owners were included: Flavio Briatore was joint 39th, with a fortune of £120 million, Bernie and Slavica Ecclestone were fifth, with £2.4 billion, and Lakshmi Mittal and family were second, with £12.5 billion.

Only Sheikh Mansour, owner of Manchester City through his investment company Abu Dhabi United Group, was richer with £15 billion. Chelsea owner Roman Abramovich was third with £7 billion, just over half of Mittal's wealth.

For Thomas, this injection of financial power into the club has shifted the goalposts: "I don't think we're doing anything different now to what we've always done, but we can't influence people who are coming into the club, like the new regime, who don't have the same understanding of its culture and history.

"Down the years, people who've sat in the boardroom at QPR have always held *A Kick up the R's* in a healthy regard – they may not like us, they may not agree with us, they may find us a pain in the arse – but there's always been that kind of respect.

"But I suspect to a couple of billionaires and a millionaire we are just a rag. I don't know how we could possibly earn that respect from them, any more than any other QPR fan could. That's clearly the problem. They just see us as people who turn up for the game.

"I keep coming back to three words when I talk about QPR – culture, history, tradition – and you cannot just step into the club and understand these things. You have to live them, experience them or at least be astute enough to acknowledge they exist. Not necessarily understand them but give them due respect.

"Or you could be as I think the new owners are, pretty damn dismissive of them. Even if we made the most impassioned plea and had QPR fans on their feet cheering and shouting, it's not going to make a blind bit of difference to these people because they're so far removed.

"Don't get me wrong, it's not an 'us and them' situation. I'd like nothing more than for Briatore, Ecclestone, Mittal or Amit Bhatia, whoever it may be, to sit down with us and say, 'Teach us about the culture. Let's sit down and have a chat about it.' But I don't think they're really interested. And I think that's really sad. All we can do is keep knocking on the door, keep chipping away.

"I do realise that sometimes we're almost preaching to the converted. Maybe if we sat down we could work out a strategy that could get the ear of the club, but that's what we're trying to do already. Whether they want to listen or not remains to be seen.

"But I think when it comes to who's pulling the ultimate power, which is Flavio ultimately, I don't think he's listening or is interested in listening. I think he's set on a course where he believes he's fundamentally right in the decisions he makes and everything else is just irrelevant to that."

Thomas believes he represents a growing feeling among the fans this season. "I think every fan at the club feels there's an increasing alienation between the supporters and the club. Look at the Oldham game [Division Two Play-Off Semi-Final, Loftus Road, 2003] and that sense of belonging and identity that existed that amazing night.

"Now what I'm hearing all the time is that I've never felt more disillusioned with the club. It's not my club anymore and I don't like what they're doing to it. And yet, it would be so simple to turn that around.

"I could have this ground full at the start of next season. But it won't be. Season tickets next season are going to dive off because, for starters, they're charging too much. There isn't this great swathe of people waiting to join the revolutionary ride to the 'promised land'. They thought that was going to happen last season, but it hasn't, so that alienation is starting to take hold now.

"People are starting to feel disillusioned. It's like watching your parents go through a divorce. You care about them but there's nothing you can do about it. You're helpless. The fanzine operates as the fans' voice if you like. All we can do is continue to put the message across, and try to make representations to the club that say, 'Look, we're not trying to tell you how to do your job, but listen to us. We're the experts.'

"It's the age-old thing that people only ever write in to the fanzine to complain. They don't write in to say how fantastic it all is, but I've got anecdotal evidence that suggests there's definitely a pattern emerging, and if it was repeated across the whole support base then I would be really worried if I was at the club.

"And that anecdotal evidence says there's an issue about cost and about no longer feeling connected to the club.

"You can spin it as much as you like, dress it up however you want, but the bottom line is the club is not a supermarket brand trying to tout for our custom. This is not a choice between ASDA and Tesco, with us thinking one is cheaper than the other. This is an emotional commitment to a football club, and that's the bit they're missing. What worries me is the drip, drip, drip effect of fans growing disillusioned.

"Every single letter I've had, and I've had dozens, has been from people saying I'm not going to renew my season ticket next season. I'll pick and choose the games I go to instead. The effect of that is it becomes easy not to go to Swansea on a Tuesday night. You need a winning side on the field and there's nothing to suggest we're going to automatically have that next season.

"I think the walk-up ticket sales this year have been very low, by which I mean somebody who decides to go to the Nottingham Forest game, for instance, and walks up on the day of the match to buy a ticket.

"They're the people I think have been missing this year. I can see that in the sales of the fanzine. For a lot of people coming to a game, part of the routine is picking up a fanzine as well, and I can notice the faces that are missing.

"I might say, 'I haven't seen you for a while,' and they might reply, 'Yeah, haven't been up for a few months now.' Before this would have been unthinkable, and it's all linked. It's what's happening on the pitch, it's the cost of going and it's the alienation from the club.

"You have to be able to read the situation. It ebbs and flows and it's never black and white, but I'm just saying, as I see it, the situation we have at the moment is not a healthy one. Not a good one.

"Before, when we were being mismanaged, fans would be angry. Now there's no need to be angry. Who can be angry about billionaires and a millionaire who want to come into your club and tart up the stadium a bit? Yes, you can be angry about the ticket prices, but people aren't angry in the same way they were when the club was about to go bust. Now there's no danger of the club going bust. It's just, what will it look like in a year from now, or two years, or five years?

"In the past, when we rattled buckets outside the stadium, people rallied round. When we were in the third division, we sang, 'We'll support you ever more,' and we did, we made record crowds in that division. But if QPR went down this season, it wouldn't be the same. Something is different. I know instinctively this is the case and most QPR fans would probably agree with me.

"I don't want this to sound anti-Briatore because I'm not that at all. But he could make such a success of this club if he embraced the core traditions. It's like buying the Tower of London and turning it into a theme park, whereas if he kept it as an historical monument he would make a lot more out of it and people wouldn't resent him for it.

"I'm not clever enough to tell you exactly how and why it's different this season, but it is. And sometimes you just can't explain something, but I'm right. I'm 100 per cent right, I know I am.

"If I'm really honest, I'm not immune from it myself. Over the last year or so, I've probably had more moments of questioning or self-doubt than ever before. It's almost, 'Is it coming to an end?'

"I have to choose my words very carefully here because I'm not wrestling with the idea of, 'Will I be here next season or not, or the season after that?' I'm sure I will because it's habit, it's love and I'm not going to desert the club now. But I suppose it's the passage of time. You can't be at the forefront of what we're doing forever.

"We've had a pretty good run with the fanzine for 20-odd years. I don't feel that we're any less relevant now. But I think it's the bits that we can't influence that are changing. In a nutshell, I'm saying to the club, 'I feel exactly the same about you, darling, but you don't feel the same about me.'

"It's that helplessness of not knowing what you can do to change it. None of us are falling out of love with QPR, but QPR, as it is being driven, is falling out of love with us. It's not the QPR we know.

"If we had a *Sliding Doors* situation – give Briatore a couple of years and see where we are, and then, if you put me in his position and turn the clock back – I would make QPR a stronger club in two years than he would.

"Not because I'm cleverer than him. Look, I drive a 200 quid car for Christ's sake. But that doesn't make him better than me. It makes him better at building businesses and having yachts. But he doesn't know QPR like I do. If I ever go to meet him, I'll call him Mr Briatore and as far as I'm concerned he has my utmost respect. But I expect to get respect back.

"I would set about reinforcing the values. I know that sounds like some sort of mantra, but it's about being open with the fans. The club could be so much more imaginative, so that it understood what nights like Oldham were all about.

"It wasn't just a play-off semi-final. It was much more emotional than that. It wasn't just a game we had to win to go down and play Cardiff in the play-off final. The ground rocked that night because it went so much deeper than that, and if you could bottle it and sell it you'd be a millionaire.

"When I talk about reinforcing the values, it sounds like pie in the sky, but I really don't think it is. It's what built this club, 120 years in the making. Briatore believes he came in and rescued us. That he saved the club. But even if we ended up AFC QPR, you can still maintain a club's history, culture and tradition.

"You can't wipe it out overnight. But what you can do is lose it over time. It can lessen and fade away. But it's out there in every pub in west London. It's out there when we're having a laugh at Man United fans on the M6. It's still out there and hasn't been lost. If you understand it, you can bring it all together.

"You have to fill the stadium first and foremost, and I honestly believe that I could do that. I'd reduce ticket prices, and it's about what that means. It says we're giving the club back to the fans, and while perhaps they wouldn't sit there and analyse it in the same way, the fans would understand it. They'd get it. It would create a feel-good factor and a ripple effect.

"This is just my opinion but I don't think I'm wrong, because it's my club and I've been involved for so long with it that I can read it."

Thomas is convinced that he speaks for a groundswell of opinion among long-serving fans at Loftus Road. But does he talk for all supporters? Are there different readings of the current situation at QPR?

Are some fans just grateful that the board is in control of the club, offering it much-needed financial security? Is that, after all, the only thing that really matters?

CHAPTER THIRTEEN

"ONE OF THE things we've learnt from the turmoil that's gone on at the club for the last 20 years is that the last person you want running the club is a fan," insists Ron Lewis, a season-ticket holder at Loftus Road for 34 years.

"They can't be rational about it. Everything that's gone wrong in our club happened when there were fans in charge, not when a ruthless bastard was in charge. The ruthless bastards aren't in the club to run it down. They can see it's got to have some kind of sustainability.

"The period that ruined it for us was the Chris Wright era. He came in as a fan, wasted tons of money, chucked his toys out of the pram and asked for his money back. Briatore clearly doesn't care about being mates with the fans, and why should he? If you're going to be mates with the people he hangs around with, why are you going to hang around the Springbok? He's not in this for the street cred . . .

"Football clubs are very important things in people's lives. While the club is still a huge part of my life, it's clearly less than it was when I was 16 or 17. There were times back then when I lived and died with the results.

"But you realise, over time, the result isn't that important.

Promotion isn't that important. For Rangers, it's much more important that there is a club here in 10 years time. We need financial security, which is what this board offers us."

Lewis, who sits in the Upper Loft, saw the cost of his season ticket go up £200 at the start of the season, which outraged him at the time. "After 34 years, I was hardly going to stop buying my season ticket, was I? But what it did do was focus my mind on what I spent my money on.

"Was I going to buy a new QPR shirt after four years since my last one? I didn't in the end, and that was £50 saved. There's probably a couple of away games I was going to go to that I haven't been to, and that's £25 a ticket, plus £25 getting there, and that's all money saved."

He says that the board obviously saw the season-ticket hike as a scheme to make extra revenue, but he was just glad that the club was financially secure after the turmoil of previous years. That for him was the all-important thing.

What he *had* noticed, though, was a distinct change of mood inside the stadium this season, which disturbed him. "I would say it's the worst atmosphere I can ever remember in the ground. Some of the relegation years were obviously very depressing, but I would say there's a nasty element to it this year.

"It's as if it's now, 'Right, you're running the club, we demand success,' and I don't ever remember a time when Rangers fans demanded success. There have been times when we've done well and hoped for success. But it's a different situation these days.

"I've noticed the change in the Upper Loft where I sit. There's this guy that's been coming along this year who sits behind me and he's terrible. He's so abusive."

In January 2009, QPR drew 1-1 with Coventry at home. They couldn't beat a team that had been reduced to 10 men in the first half after an opponent was sent off, but Dexter

Blackstock saved QPR's blushes with an equaliser three minutes from time.

"I was coming home from the Coventry match, which was obviously a terrible game, and the abuse afterwards was unbelievable," acknowledges Lewis. "I was listening to the radio phone-in on BBC London and this guy rang up to say the manager should be sacked because he hasn't got a clue.

"But do you really want to get rid of Sousa, who inherited someone else's squad mid-season and had only lost one league game at the time? Under Dowie we were hopeless. I thought that was a terrible appointment. He was having a ruck with Briatore which he was never going to win, because he was not the be-all and end-all of this club. All we were was a long-ball team. But let's give Sousa a chance.

"I think the fans' attitude has changed. I don't think we've got different fans this season, but I think there are probably a lot of fans who've come back to Loftus Road after a period of time away, expecting to see a successful side. Also, I think there were a lot of fans who had very strange expectations at the start of the season as well, who thought, 'We've got all this money, so this season is going to be completely smooth and wonderful.'

"There's a real sense of hatred from a section of the fans who are simply demanding success. People have always booed or got frustrated by certain players. But I've never ever seen the demand for success there's been this year, and the lack of patience. It's just absolutely extraordinary. I can understand why they're doing it but I can't sympathise with it."

It was a complete contrast to the atmosphere at Loftus Road during more financially turbulent times, when Ian Holloway was manager and before the current owners took over to raise expectations. "In the past, the attitude among the fans was different. We're crap, but it's *our* crap.

"It's our team and we're going to show our loyalty and be there until the end. The play-off semi-final against Oldham was the highlight of that era and was the best example of the sort of atmosphere you can generate at Loftus Road, with the pitch so tightly surrounded by the fans. You're almost on the pitch with them.

"But when fans say now, 'I'd rather be back then, when it was our club – we don't own the club anymore,' well, that's all rubbish, isn't it? I can't agree with that. Was it any more my club then than it is now?

"I went through the first 25 to 30 years of supporting Rangers when we were essentially a Premiership side. For three years we were in Division Two. We were never this tiny little lower-league club where everyone knows everyone else. We were a good club and a big club.

"OK, we didn't have the fanbase of Arsenal, but I never went to Chelsea back then and ever thought they were a bigger club than us. They were always below us in the league. Yes, they may have more history and a bigger stadium than us, but what's that got to do with it?

"I think we wrongly reinvented the period under Ian Holloway as the time when it was the 'real Rangers', and it wasn't. I always thought we were in a completely false position back then, and that at some point we would at least get ourselves back up to where we are now.

"I never saw us going down further. When Rodney Marsh said we were heading to the Conference, I never saw that at all. We were never a club with 3,000 or 4,000 fans, even at our worst points. Now this year, some people have made out that Briatore has come along and stolen our club from us, which isn't true.

"I don't feel any less of a sense of belonging now than I did when Jim Gregory was chairman in the 70's, and I don't have any more influence on the club either, because in reality no fan has any influence on the club.

"But because we were successful back then, everyone was happy. This idea, that the fans own the club, I always find a very strange thing to understand. I don't think we are blatantly just customers, because you obviously don't have the option to shop around and support another club. But at the same time, while we invest our emotions into it, we don't invest the same financial risk as the owners.

"I think Briatore wants to turn QPR into a successful club that people want to become a member of – I don't mean a football club here, but more like a nightclub or a gentlemen's club. You want to be a member of it and say, 'I'm not Chelsea, I'm QPR.'

"When Briatore came up with the stupid new crest, it did have two of the things I care most about on it. It had the hoops on it and it had 'Loftus Road' written on the badge. And I've always thought the most important things about QPR are where we play, our kit and our name.

"And everything else is transitory, isn't it? The players change, the manager changes, the owners move on. But those things should always stay the same. They're the essence of our club."

The debate about the over-expectant atmosphere and the hostility emanating from some sections of the crowd would come to a high-profile climax, during the visit of Ipswich in February 2009. The match was screened live by Sky Sports. England boss Fabio Capello, fresh from watching Chelsea's win at Aston Villa, was also present, enjoying the hospitality of fellow Italian Flavio Briatore.

Simon Skinner, who writes match reports for *QPRnet.com*, noted a tangible sense of anticipation in the air before the evening kick-off. Performances during the previous month had been impressive, including away wins at Derby and Blackpool. The team had gone 10 league games without defeat, whereas disaffected Ipswich supporters had called for the dismissal of their manager, Jim Magilton, during a pre-game midweek demonstration.

As Skinner recalls, "The atmosphere before the Ipswich game was that we had to win. We're on Sky. We're on a good run. This was a chance to show people what we're all about. Everyone wanted the play-offs so badly and the Ipswich manager Magilton had the fans on his back, and his job hanging by a thread.

"This was a chance for us to come out of the blocks and have a right go at them and we were 1-0 ahead after a couple of minutes. But that was probably the worst thing that could have happened to us."

After an early goal by young Italian striker Samuel Di Carmine, QPR proceeded to fall apart in calamitous fashion. Stand-in skipper Gavin Mahon, who was having a poor game, particularly took the brunt of the fans' frustration.

In the first-half, a shocking back header to Rangers keeper Lee Camp nearly let in Ipswich to score; in the second, his disastrous decision to dribble out of defence led to him losing possession and an Ipswich goal.

With just over an hour gone, the visitors were 1-2 ahead. Paulo Sousa had to make changes in a bid to salvage the points. Until now, Di Carmine had played up front as a lone striker in a 4-5-1 formation. Rangers fans wanted to see a second forward introduced and Mahon replaced. But defender Damien Delaney was subbed instead.

This is an extract from Simon Skinner's report for *QPRnet.com*:

Another sub appeared on the touchline, Blackstock this time. Two up front now, surely, with Mahon being taken off? Number 2? Isn't that our left-back [Delaney]? Sousa gave us two up front but now went three at the back, and with over 20 minutes left to go, it looked like tactical suicide. And so it proved, as barely three minutes after the left-back went off, Ipswich scored and I bet you can guess where from.

Quinn received the ball in midfield and flighted a superb pass over the head of Gorkss and into the path of sub Walters. The big Irishman galloped into the space Delaney was filling three minutes earlier, killed the ball with his first touch and then rifled it past Camp with his second. When Rangers next got possession, Mahon picked it up in midfield and then sprayed a beautiful 40 yards pass into the wall in front of the Paddock. There were some serious rumblings of discontent and things were only going to get worse.

Another sub appeared on the touchline, Balanta this time. A front three with Mahon being taken off? Number 18? Miller! The only man in the midfield capable of getting the ball and passing it to a team-mate was now being taken off and Mahon was still there. The crowd booed the decision whilst warmly applauding Miller off and Balanta on. The next time Mahon got the ball the atmosphere went from discontented to downright rancorous. Loud boos greeted his first touch followed by applause as the good cops tried to drown out the bad cops. I don't like seeing players booed, it serves no purpose. Yes, Mahon had been utter shite, but that isn't exactly going to gee him up is it!

The atmosphere inside the stadium was turning ugly. Sections of the crowd started chanting, "You don't know what you're doing!" in the direction of Sousa. His substitutions were being criticised, as was his preference for one striker upfront, when a lot of fans wanted to see two forwards play at home in a 4-4-2 system.

QPR lost the game 1-3 and, after the match, Sousa faced the waiting media. He said: "My message is that when we lose, we lose together, and when we win, we win together. It was not a good game for Gavin, but not just him, for some other players also. It's normal for fans to want to see their teams always win with good performances. I understand that."

He said he'd heard the criticism he'd personally received from a section of the crowd for subbing Liam Miller during the match, and not Mahon, adding, "I want to say to the fans that everyone counts in my squad. Gavin needs to have support from me, his colleagues, from my staff and especially from the fans. But also because of the shape of the team, I needed strong, physical midfielders on the pitch. If I'd taken him off at that moment, it would have created more problems."

The next home game was against Norwich City. Injured skipper Martin Rowlands tackled the booing issue head on in his programme notes, defending stand-in captain Mahon: "He gives his all for this club – day in, day out – and for him to come in for the type of criticism a small minority of you – our supporters – gave him against the Tractor Boys was nothing short of disgraceful.

"Once again, I know it was only a small group of fans that were responsible, but that doesn't make it any more excusable. By his own admission, Gav didn't have a good game, but he wasn't the only one and what good is it going to do booing him and the lads in general?"

Player and lifelong fan Lee Cook found himself in an awkward position when boos rang around the stadium: "Players do hear these things and it wasn't like this before. There's now an expectation around the place. And I've taken some stick in the changing-room, to be fair. The players look at me as if to say, 'What's up with your mates?'"

Cook knew that the fans had paid increased season ticket

prices at Loftus Road this season, and wanted to see good football on the pitch. But he also stressed that they should be wary of the negative affects of getting on the players' backs. "At home, players might feel a bit nervous on the ball and go hiding a bit, feeling that they're going to be judged. Away from home, they might feel a bit more relaxed.

"We need the support of every single person when we play at home. I want to see Loftus Road turned into a fortress, a small pitch with the fans right on top of you. What we don't want is opposing managers coming here saying, 'Let's try to get their fans on their backs.'

"For me, next season is the big one for QPR. There's a three-year plan at this club and we want to be in the Premiership. I want to be there, and I want the fans to help us get there."

Ron Lewis had sensed this over-expectant and hostile mood brewing inside Loftus Road during the weeks leading up to the Ipswich game. The sequence of events that unfolded that evening simply confirmed his worst fears: "There are two main problems at Rangers at the moment. One, we have fans with delusions of grandeur. And two, so many players in key positions are out injured.

"Akos Buzsaky and Rowan Vine are missing, add Martin Rowlands to that list of influential casualties too. I wouldn't have played Mahon because I find him such a negative player. It drives me mad how he keeps passing the ball backwards. But players are always going to make mistakes and there are fans here that will slaughter their own players.

"That was the worst atmosphere in the stadium this year. Di Carmine, a 20-year-old who I think is a decent young player, was slaughtered by a section of the fans too. 'He's not one of us,' someone said.

"These fans have absolutely no sense of realism. Then there

was the guy in the Upper Loft again, near where I sit, who is the classic 'Rangers hater'. He was offensive and abusive to players, and he proceeded to say, 'Paulo Sow-sa,' the whole game when he criticised him, which really got on my nerves.

"He had a go at Mahon and then Lee Camp in goal, who he said wasn't wanted here anymore because he'd cost us two points at Nottingham Forest the previous game. [It was a 2-2 draw at the City Ground and Camp had been on loan at Forest earlier in the season.] Why does a bloke like that go to see QPR? He clearly can't be enjoying it. And he's on the way to having a heart attack.

"We played badly against Ipswich, we were poor. Mahon had no creativity in midfield, Routledge was our best player and Miller was alright, but he can't run the midfield all on his own.

"I don't think the problem is the system. It would work well with the right creative players. The more games I watch, the more I think that, if we had Buzsaky and Vine playing, we'd be 10 points better off and in third or fourth place in the table.

"Yet fans are calling for the manager to be sacked – absolutely nuts! The best thing they can do is get behind the manager and take the long-term view. It's not the style of football that's the problem. It's the fact that our most creative players are all injured. I just wish we could have got Gareth Ainsworth onto the pitch as a sub. He was always a player that would go on and turn a game."

Dave Thomas, editor of *A Kick up the R's*, was shocked by the treatment of Mahon and studied how it manifested itself during the game: "The interesting point is how it built up. First a few people chanced their arm and booed him.

"Then there were a lot more people joining in. Then, the next time he got the ball, some people tentatively cheered him. Then a lot more cheered him. And that, for me was fantastic, because it completely fucked off the boo-ers.

"I'm not a boo-er myself. He doesn't deserve that and I don't believe that the people who were booing were truly representative of the fans. When fans started cheering Mahon there were no more boos because they'd been put in their place, good and proper.

"It was four touches of the ball – tentative boos, a lot of booing, tentative cheering, a lot of cheering. It was a strange episode, like a little vignette within the game."

Simon Skinner took a slightly different view of the booing and cheering episode: "I think the Rangers fans are hard to please – some of them say, 'Go on then, entertain me.' And I think this season's atmosphere at the ground goes back to the season ticket prices. People expected more for the price they are paying and they're not getting it.

"Booing Mahon was obviously wrong, but when some people started clapping him to balance out boos that made the situation even more bizarre. I agree you shouldn't boo a player, but don't applaud him either for just trapping a ball and passing it. That's what he should be doing. The whole thing was like a pantomime – just bizarre, really bizarre."

For Thomas, this defeat proved a definitive turning point in the season: "My view is that the realisation hit home that we weren't going up and we just weren't good enough to go up. The subtext to that is a lot of the anger came from those who believed the hype and bought into the idea that we were going to go up.

"It came to a head, and when a mood spreads it can have a snowball effect. There was a lot of anger around. That one performance was a shambles. Any team with hopes of going up would not produce a performance as disorganised and as lacking in every attribute you need to go up.

"I think the makeup of the supporters in the ground has to be taken into account. A lot of the old guard, fans who've been going regularly for 10, 20 or 30 years, have reluctantly thrown in the towel.

"But I think there is a new generation of fans here now, perhaps lapsed fans that have come back this year. Clearly, if some are staying away, others are going in their place because the team's not playing in front of empty stadiums, is it? They've wandered back to see what's going on and they're the ones who've bought into it all. Suddenly, they got a bit angry.

"If we've got 14,000 fans in the ground, I would be very interested to know how many were there five years ago. And I suspect a lot less than you'd imagine. Of the 10,000 season tickets that have been sold this season, I think there's a lot of new or returning fans in that.

"I see loads of fans at away games who don't bother going to home games anymore. In my opinion, I think the turnover is much more that you might expect, and that percentage is influencing the angry mood."

Lifelong QPR fan and former player Marc Bircham also watched the drama unfold during the Ipswich match: "Gavin Mahon was the first QPR captain I'd heard being booed since Karl Ready [in the 90's].

"QPR fans aren't like that, they don't boo their own. But I think they cracked. I think Gavin's a really nice geezer who just happened to have a bad game. It happens."

Former QPR manager Ian Holloway was at Loftus Road, working as a pundit on the Sky Sports coverage of the dire proceedings. Bircham spoke to his former gaffer after the final whistle:

"I suspect the wages have quadrupled since his time here, but Ian Holloway said that if he had the 11 players that played Ipswich and his best 11 players from when he was manager, he'd probably only take two from the current 11," Bircham explains.

"He'd probably need a goalie and he said he'd probably need a right-back – maybe a cover for centre-half. But he'd keep the midfield of me, Gaz [Gareth Ainsworth], Rolly [Martin Rowlands] and Cookie [Lee Cook], with Kevin Gallen and Paul Furlong upfront. Perhaps a fit Akos Buzsaky or Rowan Vine would come in, but there are not many changes.

"And that was a team when we had no money. Would I rather be playing then or now? I liked the team I played in then. I'd like the money they're on now. But I think we were punching above our weight back then and we were better than some people gave us credit for at the time."

After the Ipswich debacle, QPR failed to win any of the next four games – there were two draws and two defeats. The day after a 0-0 draw with Sheffield United in early March 2009, the press speculated about the future of Sousa, who had now gone seven games without a win. Reports suggested that Paul Ince, dismissed by Blackburn in December 2008, was being lined up to replace him. But these rumours were quickly and strenuously denied by QPR's sporting director, Gianni Paladini.

"There is absolutely, categorically not a shred of truth in it," he insisted. "I have not spoken to Paul Ince and neither have Flavio or Bernie. There is absolutely no way he will take over at QPR and no way it was even discussed."

Ince had been linked with QPR following the departure of former first team coach Luigi De Canio at the end of the previous season, before the job went to Iain Dowie.

Paladini added: "Even if the thought had occurred to me that he should be QPR's manager – which it didn't – I don't have the power to make that decision. That decision lies with the owners and I know for a fact that they want to keep Paulo Sousa."

Bircham thought that the last thing QPR needed was more upheaval. "We're a club in limbo right now," he said. "We're in the middle of a time of change and how it's going to end up, I don't know. They've got to give Sousa a year in charge.

"He probably knew next to nothing about the Championship when he came here. Give him a pre-season to work on his ideas and get them right. Work on a formation and a team that can go up next year. Every good team needs stable foundations."

Simon Skinner agrees that what the club needs most is stability. "Under this board we've had six people in charge – John Gregory, Mick Harford, Luigi De Canio, Iain Dowie, Gareth Ainsworth and Paulo Sousa. But these constant changes have got to stop. Even if the manager isn't doing well and the crowd are clamouring for him to be sacked, and we will be if a few results don't go our way, the board has got to stick with Sousa for another season.

"I also think they have got to get their cheque book out in the summer. If they're expecting fans to pay £600 for a season ticket, they've got to reveal what that £600 is buying, a striker for £5 million or something.

"To go up, you've got to find that 25-goal-a-season striker. Will they get a striker from the Premiership who'll come down to the Championship, or pick off a striker from another team that misses out on promotion? We'll see what the options are. But I think they have got to buy a guaranteed goal-scorer, we're simply crying out for one.

"I think most fans would say the play-offs are way off now. This season's finished as far as I'm concerned. Let's concentrate on next season and get that core of the side settled and playing well together. Find a formation that works and that will get us up into the Premiership in a year's time."

After the Ipswich defeat QPR dropped to 11th place in the table, a position they failed to rise above for the rest of February and the whole of March. They were in 11th place – the epitome of mid-table obscurity – for eight of the nine weeks until the start of April, apart from one week when they dropped to 12th.

The campaign seemed to be drawing to a dull and uneventful close. QPR was not going up, but there was no threat of relegation either. However, the Loftus Road faithful had another shock in store.

There was one last dramatic twist to the season, which would leave the QPR board searching for yet another manager. Despite whatever anyone had said, Paulo Sousa's days in W12 were numbered.

FEBRUARY

PAULO SOUSA AS FIRST TEAM COACH

Nottingham Forest 2-2 QPR
7 February 2009
Attendance: 25,859
Visiting Rangers fans: 2,052
Scorer: Alberti (2)
Table: 9th with 47 points

QPR 1-3 Ipswich Town
21 February 2009
Attendance: 13,904
Scorer: Di Carmine
Table: 11th with 47 points

Cardiff City 0-0 QPR
25th February 2009
Attendance: 17,340
Visiting Rangers fans: 378
Table: 11th with 48 points

Barnsley 2-1 QPR
28 February 2009
Attendance: 11,614
Visiting Rangers fans: 782
Scorer: Delaney
Table: 11th with 48 points

MARCH

PAULO SOUSA AS FIRST TEAM COACH

QPR 0-1 Norwich City
3 March 2009
Attendance: 13,533
Table: 11th with 48 points

QPR 0-0 Sheffield United
7 March 2009
Attendance: 13,718
Table: 11th with 49 points

Doncaster 2-0 QPR
10 March 2009
Attendance: 10,223
Visiting Rangers fans: 660
Table: 11th with 49 points

Southampton 0-0 QPR
14 March 2009
Attendance: 18,691
Visiting Rangers fans: 2,490
Table: 12th with 50 points

QPR 1-0 Swansea City
17 March 2009
Attendance: 12,288
Scorer: Leigertwood
Table: 11th with 53 points

QPR 2-1 Bristol City
21 March 2009
Attendance: 14,059
Scorers: Lopez, Taarabt
Table: 11th with 56 points

CHAPTER FOURTEEN

AS APRIL BEGAN, mathematically it was still possible. But in reality dreams of the play-offs were well and truly over. With six games to go, the club was languishing in mid-table. It was in 11th place and seven points behind Cardiff City in sixth spot.

But if anyone thought the season was going to gently peter out, they couldn't have been further from the truth. Events behind-the-scenes at Loftus Road were about to take centre stage once again, as the season reached its dramatic climax.

When Crystal Palace visited Loftus Road for a London derby, the third and final local derby of the season, what was happening off the pitch proved far more interesting than the dire, goalless draw being played out upon it.

Over a period of just six days, events would unfold at a breakneck pace with shocking consequences for Paulo Sousa. Even by this season's rollercoaster standards, it was a remarkable week at the club.

The Palace match itself was not without controversy for Sousa. He was sent to the stands in first-half stoppage time for passionately remonstrating on the touchline about the way striker Samuel Di Carmine was treated by Palace defender Claude Davis. It was the first time he'd ever been banished from the dugout by an official. Fans in the South Africa Road stand could see him being held back in his technical area. He raged with anger as blood streamed from Di Carmine's nose.

In the second half, the much-anticipated return to first-team action of striker Rowan Vine took place after a year on the sidelines with a serious leg fracture. He came on as a substitute for the last quarter of an hour to a rapturous welcome from the home fans. They'd missed his undoubted talent on the pitch at Loftus Road.

But as well as chanting Vine's name, Q Block was also heard singing the praises of striker Dexter Blackstock, who the previous week had joined Nottingham Forest on loan until the end of the season – a move that baffled most fans because Blackstock was QPR's top scorer, with 12 goals.

In the post-match interviews, Sousa stunned reporters by indicating that it wasn't his decision to loan Blackstock to Nottingham Forest: "I gave the players two days off after the Bristol City game and when I came back Gianni Paladini told me he had an agreement [for Blackstock] to go on loan. It is a decision for the board and only they can answer it."

Rowan Vine told reporters he was bewildered by the news. "There doesn't seem to be much need to let your top goalscorer go for the last month of the season. I don't see the sense in it but it's not my decision. I was just surprised it's happened."

But the events surrounding the Crystal Palace game were only half the story. A subplot had already begun unfolding the evening before, at Heathrow Airport, when Sousa returned to the UK after a short break.

In what initially appeared an entirely innocent meeting, Sousa chatted with a QPR fan who spotted him at the airport. During their conversation, it is alleged Sousa talked about the fitness of two players in the first-team squad. This brief encounter, and what it was claimed he had said, would haunt him during the days to come.

After Saturday's Palace game, Sousa's week began to spiral out of control:

Sunday 5 April: Sousa's post-match comments about Blackstock become the game's main talking point in the Sunday papers. Reporters dissect the remarks and find it difficult to understand how a loan decision can be made without the approval of the first team coach.

Monday 6 April: The contract of Bruno Oliviera, the Portuguese assistant coach Sousa brought to Loftus Road, is ended. The Portuguese media speculate that Sousa will be the next person to leave the club.

Tuesday 7 April: A post appears on the official QPR message board, as well as the message board of *We Are the Rangers Boys* and other websites. The fan who met Sousa at Heathrow Airport on Friday quotes what Sousa is alleged to have said about the fitness of two players.

The post is up on *We Are the Rangers Boys* for about 36 hours. People who initially reply are unsure about its validity. On a message board people can, in theory, say anything, so controversial posts about players are not always believed.

But this person then posts a photograph of himself with Sousa in an attempt to prove that the conversation really took place. Moderators of the message board initially look at the comments and do not realise the full extent of what is about to happen.

Thursday 9 April: The organisers of the website receive calls from the club, as officials try to get to the bottom of where the message about the players' fitness came from and the truth behind it. Fans involved with the website can only assume this is part of a wider discussion about Sousa at the club.

By 8pm that evening, Sousa's contract was terminated for giving away "confidential and sensitive information". A statement on the club's official website read: "Queens Park Rangers Football Club has today had to terminate Paulo Sousa's employment with the club with immediate effect

"It came to the club's attention that Mr Sousa had, without authority, divulged highly confidential and sensitive information. The club, with legal advice, responded in this way to protect its position. Player/coach Gareth Ainsworth will take caretaker charge on a temporary basis, from now until the end of the season."

Pete Davies, one of the organisers behind the *We Are the Rangers Boys* website, inadvertently found himself at the centre of the storm: "I was shopping in Somerfield that Thursday evening when I got a call from someone at the official supporters' club, saying that they wanted me to go on Sky Sports to give my opinion on what had happened that evening. I decided not to do it.

"I got home to see it all on Sky Sports News at 10 o'clock and it was like watching *Crimewatch*. I was getting calls left, right and centre about it, and there I was with my shopping bags. The presenter was saying, 'We're going to get to the bottom of this, find out exactly what this breach of confidential information is.'"

Davies reckoned he knew what the breach might be and didn't enjoy the prospect of being part of a headline-making story. He was half expecting his own mugshot to pop up on screen, with Sky Sports News presenter Jim White asking, "Have you seen this man?"

But the sports media believed at this stage that the 'information' referred solely to Sousa's post-match comments about Blackstock after the Crystal Palace game. They seemed to know nothing about the postings on message boards, as the club statement didn't specify any details.

"They went through the normal process of reading out QPR fans' emails and a member of the Independent R's went on the phone to the two presenters instead," explains Davies, who is not a fan of Sousa's style of football.

"It was fair to say the major consensus was that Paulo Sousa should have been given more time. That was not my view, but that had nothing to do with the posting staying up or being deleted. In fact, the poster of the message claims to have done it to promote Paulo Sousa and not discredit him."

"To be honest, all the talk in the media about it being just about Sousa's comments about Blackstock after the Palace game was a relief. It helped take the pressure off me slightly."

As news about Sousa spread that Thursday evening, stunned Rangers fans were contacting each other with updates. Barrie Kelly heard about Sousa leaving when he picked up a message on his mobile. "My dad left the message for me, telling me what he'd heard, and my first reaction was great surprise. 'What's going on now?' I thought. I went straight onto Sky Sports News where it was the top story.

"When Dowie was sacked it didn't seem to get the same reaction, but this time everyone was saying, 'What are QPR doing?' 'What is this plan? Is there a four-year or a four-minute plan?' People were just saying, 'Why?'

"Watching the TV, I just had so many unanswered questions. Sousa going – couldn't understand it. Blackstock going – couldn't understand it."

But the Blackstock issue and the revelation about Oliviera leaving earlier in the week told him that everything wasn't well at W12. "After I read about Oliviera leaving I thought Sousa would go, to be honest, which is ridiculous, absolutely ridiculous. Why should we be thinking that? OK, the results weren't great, but they weren't that bad either.

"For Blackstock, our top scorer by a margin, to be loaned out to Nottingham Forest – who were relegation fodder – for the rest of the season, just made no sense on any level, and it's never really been adequately explained to my liking why he went.

"You have to fill in the gaps yourself – maybe Rowan Vine's coming back and they don't think they need him. I actually thought they might be bringing in another striker on loan to replace Blackstock.

"You just assume that Sousa is part of the decision-making process and he's lined someone else up, but for it to go silent made no sense whatsoever. It's as if the club had given up on the play-offs there and then. Whether it's true or not, that's the impression you're left with.

"But at the end of it all, what we do know is that Sousa's gone, Gareth Ainsworth's in charge again, no one seems to care too much about the last few games of the season and it feels as if we're going to have to start all over again in August.

"Having said all that though, are we going to start again in the same way? Because this season may have left some scars that could take time to heal. Briatore's come in for a lot of stick, more so than anyone else on the board.

"On one hand, I agree with him. It's his money, so he can do what he likes with the club he owns. He saved it from going under, and I'm forever grateful for that.

"But what I don't agree with is that, if a manager has a bad run of games, you feel like he's going to pull the trigger and get rid of him. It's tried and tested that an approach like that wins you nothing in football. The majority of successful teams have managers who've been there for a long period of time."

Accusing fingers were pointed at the board. On Friday 10 April, the day after Sousa's contract was terminated, the club released a statement on its official website from Dexter

Blackstock's agent, Eric Walters, in a bid to clear up the confusion about the player's loan deal. It also deflected some of the criticism the board was receiving:

> *Dexter was unhappy at QPR for some time, as he had only started six of a possible 21 fixtures. He wasn't even on the bench for QPR's home fixture against Bristol City and seeing as he was the club's top goalscorer, Dexter was unhappy about this situation.*
>
> *A few clubs approached me for Dexter, including Nottingham Forest. I spoke with Gianni Paladini and he advised me that we needed to clear this with Paulo Sousa. Paulo came back from Portugal on March 26th at lunchtime.*
>
> *Dexter discussed the situation with Paulo, and he didn't say anything to Dexter about the possibility of him staying with QPR. At 4.00pm on March 26th 2009, Dexter signed the paperwork to complete his loan transfer to Nottingham Forest.*

The next home game for QPR was against Sheffield Wednesday on Easter Monday, four days after Sousa's job came to an end. On the Sunday before the game, Sousa broke his silence. He defended his character and professionalism: "I believe that Mr Briatore, like me, has always had the club's best interests at heart and I would like to thank him for giving me my first chance to manage in England. I hope that my integrity and honesty are not brought into question as I have always sought to act with both during my career."

Barrie Kelly felt a bit sorry for Sousa, who he believed had always come across as genuine and trustworthy. He also feared that a young, ambitious manager with the potential to succeed had slipped through QPR's hands.

As kick-off on Easter Monday approached, Kelly said, "It's going to be an odd atmosphere today, but I don't think anybody is particularly angry. I don't think Sousa has been here long enough for there to be anger. And I think the fans have become used to changing managers at QPR by now.

"You won't have Rangers fans at the game today shouting, 'Board out!' You don't really want billionaires to bail out as a rule, do you? But apathy's not a great thing either. And there's also another thing I fear, that Briatore might just walk away. That the money might walk away from the club if we don't get up into the Premiership within two years. That's my biggest worry.

"I'm sane enough to know that the most important thing, above all else that's going on right now, is that the club is financially secure. After all we've been through as a club in recent years, we've all got to be thankful for that.

"But I'm not happy right now about what's happening at my club or the path we're on. At the end of last season, we played West Brom at home, there were rumours of Zinedine Zidane coming to the club, there was a new crest, and we were all looking forward to the future.

"Nearly a year on, there just isn't the same excitement. Not today anyway. A lot has happened since that West Brom game and it feels like we're a bit scarred by it all."

Pete Davies, who had been dragged into the Sousa message board controversy, had second thoughts about turning up to the Sheffield Wednesday game at all. In the fallout of Sousa's departure, he had come under fire from fans who believed his website had contributed to the problems. "Going to the home game against Sheffield Wednesday was the most stressful I have felt for a very long time," he said.

"The night before, I had contemplated not going. One or two people were issuing threats on various websites. I then thought to myself, I had nothing to hide and should not be feeling guilty. I was not the one who had posted the conversation that allegedly took place, but apart from a small section of boos from the R Block [the seating area next to Q Block, where Pete sits] and one fan shouting out obscenities, the day passed by without incident.

"But that's the power of fans' message boards. They're a forum for fans to have their say and talk about the issues affecting their club. But when things go bad, it's very bad."

It was common knowledge among regulars on the message boards that Davies wasn't a Sousa fan, so he believed he'd become an easy scapegoat. "I was the perfect one. A person who is known as an obsessive poster and I was always making clear my frustrations regarding the games I watched, the 0-0 draws and going to places like Doncaster and Barnsley to see our club perform poorly."

On the day of the Sheffield Wednesday match, considering all that had happened during a tumultuous week, things seemed quite normal outside the stadium a couple of hours before kick-off.

The players arrived at about 1pm, all stopping to sign autographs outside the players' entrance in South Africa Road. In the club shop early fans hunted for end-of-season bargains. Next season there would be a new home kit, so this season's version was on sale at half-price.

There were also racks of player photos on sale for £3.99. Most of these were of the current star names that had just been signing autographs outside, but there were a few surprises. Photos of old boss Iain Dowie were still available for 50p each, while a full rack of Paulo Sousa photos had no price on them at all. Their new value was the topic of much speculation. "That'll be 10p each then, will it?" said one shopper.

Life carried on as normal in many ways, but one thing had

been lost during the previous week that could never be replaced. If one single moment summed up the traditions of QPR – and had become an iconic image for fans of the club – it was the sight of the 1967 League Cup trophy being lifted by club captain Mike Keen.

That team, inspired by Rodney Marsh, had put QPR on the football map, and the image of Keen with the trophy on the Wembley turf came to symbolise their staggering achievement. Third-division QPR had overcome a two-goal halftime deficit to beat first-division West Bromwich Albion 3-2 and secure the club's only major silverware.

Less than 48 hours before the 2008-09 season's Sheffield Wednesday match – which would quickly acquire its own significance to the fans because of Sousa's departure – Mike Keen had died aged 69, after suffering a short illness. Keen had made 393 appearances for Rangers, scoring 39 goals. The sad news of this death put a sombre, reflective complexion on the week's events.

A couple of minutes before the match, a statement from the board about the termination of Paulo Sousa's contract was read out over the loudspeaker to angry boos from the crowd. But when Mike Keen's memory was honoured directly before kick-off, those same fans acted completely differently.

Keen's family requested that his life be remembered by a minute's applause – rather than silence – and the respect and pride that echoed around Loftus Road for those 60 seconds brought tears to the eyes of grown men. As the minute's applause came to an end, a passionate roar enveloped all four sides of the stadium. It was as if a week's pent-up frustration and tension were released in that one moment

As Barrie Kelly says: "Mike Keen's minute applause was very touching – that was all about the history and traditions of this club. He was our Bobby Moore raised aloft on players' shoulders, the only QPR player to lift a trophy at Wembley. The booing which took place when the statement was read out was really the only bad feedback the board got from the fans on the day, and rightly so – a statement is so formal.

"But after that minute's applause, from where I was sitting in the South Africa Road stand anyway, it felt like the fans got behind the team. There was lots of applause and encouragement for the players. I heard Q Block singing, 'We want our Rangers back,' at one point, but I couldn't hear a lot of anti-board chanting.

"If Mike Keen symbolised one thing over all else, it was that this club is bigger than a board or a manager. And I think that's what the fans got behind on the day. "

The last time Gareth Ainsworth had taken control of QPR, after the sacking of Iain Dowie, he inspired one of the club's best performances of the season, beating table-toppers Birmingham City 1-0 at a snowy Loftus Road, despite being reduced to 10 men before halftime. This time he elicited a similarly impressive reaction. QPR played slick, attractive, flowing football. They dominated the first half, yet were losing 0-1 to an own goal by Gavin Mahon against the run of play.

When the second half began, QPR went 0-2 down to a disputed penalty. The irony of the score would not have been lost on the more knowledgeable fans in the crowd: the team that Mike Keen led to victory in the 1967 League Cup Final were 0-2 down at halftime before they came back in the second half to win 3-2.

"If the score stayed two nil to Wednesday," said Kelly at the time, "the board would really have got it in the neck. But then Rowan Vine came on as a sub, Wayne Routledge ran through the whole opposition defence and Vine tapped in to score. Everyone was ecstatic and the comeback began.

"It just became one of those great games for fans, because Rangers were on the rampage. It doesn't happen too often anymore, but when it does it feels great. Mahon was the inspirational skipper and got an inspirational equaliser, and Damion Stewart got the winner with only minutes to go. The marvellous comeback was complete." From 0-2 down QPR won 3-2, just like Mike Keen's side in 1967.

"All the team looked good and Ainsworth's gutsy, determined attitude was everywhere on the pitch. The irony of the timing of Mike Keen's passing, the fact that this side came back like his side did to win 3-2 and the quality of the performance we've seen today, it just highlights the history of this club and its importance to the fans who've been going week in, week out, all their lives. This history gives a club its integrity and respect.

"After the past week of turmoil, I think fans will probably choose to forget Sousa now and look to next season with fresh hope. We do it every year. It's the only reason you keep on coming back here for more torture."

Ainsworth was full of praise for his players after the game: "It was down to a fantastic bunch of lads in the dressing room. We dominated the first half and could have been three or four up. All the raised voices at halftime came from Sheffield Wednesday's dressing room.

"We kept calm, knew we were doing the right things and, although I had a little flutter at two-nil down, I still had faith."

One bit of good news revealed before the Sheffield Wednesday game was that season ticket prices had been reduced for the 2009-10 campaign, reflecting the economic downturn. One of the big contentions all season at Loftus Road had been the increase in season-ticket prices for the 2008-09 campaign. In the Upper Loft, prices had gone up by £200.

But this time around, tickets renewed before 17 May 2009

would see a five-per cent reduction in the price, while under-eights would be free in certain areas of the stadium. After 18 May 2009, the five-per cent reduction would be replaced by one of two-and-a-half per cent, reflecting the reduction in VAT earlier in the year. Ticket prices were effectively frozen.

This decision, which the club said was made after discussions with fans, was greeted as "a welcome concession" and "a step in the right direction" by *A Kick up the R's*, which had campaigned long and hard for cuts. "But it's completely outrageous that no less than 14 Premiership clubs are still offering cheaper season tickets than QPR, many substantially so," added the fanzine.

Two days after the uplifting victory over Sheffield Wednesday, chairman Flavio Briatore spoke exclusively to the official QPR website for the first time about some of the big issues affecting the club.

He rubbished claims in the media that he'd interfered with Paulo Sousa's team selection, telling him which side to choose when first team coach. "That is incorrect. Paulo picked the team all the time. As a board, we spoke about wanting to see QPR play a more attacking, aggressive brand of football, in a 4-4-2 formation, and he promised us he would do that.

"There were two incidents which disappointed us. When we beat Preston North End before Christmas, Paulo made six changes for the next match and we only drew at Charlton Athletic, who were bottom of the league.

"And against Ipswich Town, he stuck to a 4-5-1 formation, when we were at home, and that is when we became very disappointed. I was very surprised to see Damion Stewart on the bench and Radek Cerny not involved for that match.

"But I'd like to repeat, I never once told Paulo, or any other coach for that matter, which team to pick."

Briatore said that on reflection, he was happy with the

progress the club had made this season. Sixty points on the board, which hadn't been achieved by QPR at this level for many years, and the team had taken points off all the top eight sides in the division except Burnley.

The board had invested more than £34m into the club since the takeover, he said, signing 17 players including Akos Buzsaky, Rowan Vine, Lee Cook, Wayne Routledge, Kaspars Gorkss, Matthew Connolly and Radek Cerny, who provided the spine of the current side.

He added that the £10m ABC loan was dealt with, which meant that the future of Loftus Road was safe (the ground had been used as security against the loan that had crippled the club for many years).

Briatore also revealed that he was fully aware the board had been booed before the Sheffield Wednesday game. "It was only a small minority of supporters who booed, but naturally it disappoints me. The fact is, though, we saved the club when it was within minutes of going under. If it wasn't for us, this club would not be here. That is a fact," he told the QPR website.

"Furthermore, when we arrived here, we had nobody behind us, but now we are only looking towards the top. It is similar to at Renault. When we arrived we were last on the grid, and we progressed to the very top. That is what we want to happen at QPR.

"No one likes being booed, but we know we are doing the right things for the long-term future of this club and we, the board of directors, are unanimous on that. This is a very expensive hobby for us and we have already invested significant sums into the club.

"But we enjoy the moments when the supporters are behind us in the adventure. That is why we are involved, to bring joy to the fans.

"If we were fighting against relegation, I could understand the booing. But we are making positive strides in our four-year programme. This was the first full year and we are a comfortable top-half side and have a very strong squad, which is improving all the time, ahead of next season.

"If the supporters don't support us, the project won't work, so all I can ask is you come out and show your support.

"When the stadium is full, there is no better place to watch football. With your support – both home and away – we believe we can keep progressing and one day reach the Premier League.

"If we see that support, we will, of course, do our part by investing more in the future."

APRIL

PAULO SOUSA AS FIRST TEAM COACH

QPR 0-0 Crystal Palace
4 April 2009
Attendance: 15,234
Table: 10th with 57 points

APRIL/MAY

GARETH AINSWORTH AS CARETAKER MANAGER

Burnley 1-0 QPR
11 April 2009
Attendance: 15,058
Visiting Rangers fans: 364
Table: 10th with 57 points

QPR 3-2 Sheffield Wednesday
13 April 2009
Attendance: 13,742
Scorers: Vine, Mahon, Stewart
Table: 10th with 60 points

Wolves 1-0 QPR
18 April 2009
Attendance: 27,511
Visiting Rangers fans: 760
Table: 10th with 60 points

QPR 0-0 Plymouth Argyle
25th April 2009
Attendance: 14,779
Table: 11th with 61 points

Preston North End 2-1 QPR
3 May 2009
Attendance: 18,264
Scorer: Agyemang
Table: 11 with 61 points

CHAPTER FIFTEEN

AFTER A FORTNIGHT of theatre at Loftus Road that verged at times on Shakespearean tragedy, it was inevitable that the final three games of the campaign would prove a complete anticlimax. The season was effectively over for QPR and attention turned to who would be first team coach next season.

The names mentioned for the vacant post ranged from former England coach Sven-Goran Eriksson to Sir Alex Ferguson's son, Darren, whose Peterborough side had just been promoted to the Championship, and from former Chelsea coach Luiz Felipe Scolari to the return of former QPR boss Luigi De Canio. But nothing would be decided before the end of the season.

The last home game, a 0-0 draw with Plymouth, was instantly forgettable. This was the eleventh goalless draw QPR had played out this season, which summed up the whole campaign in many ways – solid at the back, but a severe lack of goals upfront.

This was also reflected in the Player of the Year awards dinner later that night at the five-star Radisson Edwardian Heathrow Hotel, where defenders received all the plaudits. Tough-tackling Jamaican defender Damion Stewart, 28, reigned supreme as he beat fellow defender Kaspars Gorkss and goalkeeper Radek Cerny to both the Supporters' Player of the Year and the Ray

Jones Players' Player of the Year awards. Another defender, England Under-21 international Matthew Connolly, won the Daphne Biggs Supporters' Young Player of the Year Award.

(While Cerny missed out on an award on the night, he would later be named as joint winner of the Championship's Golden Glove Award 2008/09, which was awarded to the goalkeeper who kept most clean sheets over a season. His stats were 19 clean sheets from 47 appearances in all competitions, and he shared the award with Sheffield United's Paddy Kenny.)

The fact that all the player of the year awards were being competed for by players who defended the QPR goal was highly significant. It was clear to fans that QPR had to improve the forward line to benefit from this impressive last line of defence. This was the sole topic of conversation after the Plymouth game. Fans wanted to see the board spend several millions, if necessary, to purchase a striker who could guarantee 20-plus goals a season.

Ironically perhaps, the next day the *Sunday Times* Rich List 2009 was announced. It revealed that QPR co-owner Lakshmi Mittal's family had seen its wealth more than halved during the economic downturn, from £27.7bn in 2008 to £10.8bn in 2009. He was now the 21st richest man in the world, but still the richest person resident in the UK, way ahead of the next richest resident. (That was Chelsea owner Roman Abramovich, in 39th place in the world, with a fortune of £7bn down from £11.7bn.)

The goalless draw against Plymouth was in the middle of two away fixtures which triggered a distinct sense of déjà vu, reminding both the board and the fans exactly what success on the pitch looked like – if only from a distance. Twelve months before, QPR had played West Brom when the West Midlands side clinched the title at Loftus Road and were promoted to the Premiership.

Despite watching their opponents win promotion, the widespread belief among Rangers fans that day was that such an achievement was within their reach next season. The QPR faithful were filled with confidence for the future, but, as similar scenarios played out not just once but twice, in the space of three weeks, these same fans began to feel less positive.

When Wolves beat QPR by a single goal in a tight game, a 25th goal of the season for the Championship's top scorer Sylvan Ebanks-Blake, they booked their place back in the top tier of English football. R's fans could only look on with envy as the home fans invaded the Molineux turf to celebrate after the final whistle.

Two weeks later, it was a similar story.

This time, Preston North End beat Rangers by two goals to one at their Deepdale ground, to snatch the final play-off place from under the noses of an off-form Cardiff City. Again, Rangers fans felt like they'd stumbled uninvited into someone else's party.

It was becoming a habit, and a sense of wasted opportunities prevailed.

The 2008-09 season had begun with a new first team coach and high hopes of the play-offs, but ended only with opposing fans and players enjoying that achievement instead. QPR finished the season in 11th position with 61 points, 13 points behind Preston North End in sixth.

The statistics revealed that the team had won 12 games at home, which compared quite well with other sides in the division. The automatically-promoted sides Wolves and Birmingham City had won only a few more, with 15 and 14 home victories respectively.

But QPR's away form was awful: only three away wins in the league all season. Only two sides in the whole Championship had away results as bad as that, and they were both relegated – Norwich, who also won three games away, while Charlton managed just two.

These statistics would not have impressed the board, as it

reflected on the season and pondered who should be the next first team coach.

On 3 June 2009, the board unveiled the new man in whom it would invest its hopes for the club. Former Ipswich boss Jim Magilton was named as the new manager, agreeing a two-year deal, with John Gorman as his assistant.

Fans noted with interest on message boards that his new position was manager, not first team coach. They wondered if this change of title would prove significant, if he would have a wider brief than his immediate predecessors.

In a further irony, when the new fixtures for the 2009-10 season were revealed a fortnight later, Magilton learnt that his first game in charge would be at Loftus Road, against a Blackpool side managed by Rangers old boy Ian Holloway – the manager who probably best symbolised life before the takeover.

On 8 August 2009, QPR began the 2009-10 campaign with a new man at the helm and fresh new hopes of promotion to the promised land of the Premiership. The club was back where it started.

It was QPR's Groundhog Day.

EPILOGUE

A SEASON IS a hell of a long time in football.

At the end of the 2007-08 campaign, Flavio Briatore was voted the most popular chairman in London in a poll of 3,000 fans for the London Football Report 2008. This reflected the gratitude of Rangers fans for making the club financially secure and transforming its fortunes.

But the story of QPR has moved on somewhat since then. Its narrative has seen numerous twists and turns.

In many ways, the story of QPR is a tale of football today. A club on the brink of financial collapse becomes the richest in the world, as the club and its fans struggle to define its new identity. This new identity has to somehow encapsulate the history and traditions of a club followed by generations of working-class west Londoners, but also to find itself at ease with its newfound wealth and the baggage that comes with it.

Was Chelsea ever the same club after it was bought by Roman Abramovich? Obviously not. How about Blackburn Rovers, after local steel baron Jack Walker invested his millions into the club he loved and effectively bought his way to the Premiership title in 1995? Again, no. Blackburn Rovers was perceived differently by other fans, and the view that Rovers fans had of themselves probably changed too. It was a club with new expectations, new horizons.

When I grew up in the 70's I was very fortunate. Inspired by Stan Bowles and Gerry Francis, QPR was the most exciting and flamboyant football team in the country. My hooped dreams were brought to life as the club chased the league title and embarked on a European adventure in the UEFA Cup

Today, my two sons – aged seven and four – have hooped dreams all of their own. They have a poster of Rowan Vine on their bedroom wall; they know that Lee Cook also grew up as a QPR fan just like them, and they can't wait to see Akos Buzsaky thrilling the crowds at Loftus Road again.

I see in them the future of this club and, despite all that's happened during a bruising 2008-09 season, I still believe it's going to be a bright one.

The people who own our club today spell millions with a 'b'. You don't become a hugely successful businessman unless you learn from your mistakes, and I think they've endured a stark learning curve. One day QPR will become an established Premiership outfit again, because I don't believe the current board can be seen to fail on this high-profile project. They have to succeed in their stated aim.

But the question that every QPR fan is asking as the 2009-10 season begins is: can Jim Magilton, as manager, lead QPR to the promised land of the Premiership? I would also like to know if he's earned his first aid badge yet, because there are gaping wounds around the club that are in desperate need of attention.

I'm sure everyone reading this book has their own opinion as to what happened during the 2008-09 season, the personalities to blame and the improvements that need to be made. All I've tried to do is document the unfolding story of the season.

But during my research and interviews – ranging from Alan

Johnson in the House of Commons to Marc Bircham in a pie and mash shop on Portobello Road – one thing has become abundantly clear to me. This club is incredibly important to people's lives.

In so many ways it's a village club, anchored in the community of west London. But, as the cost of property in areas like Shepherds Bush, Acton, Hammersmith and Notting Hill has gone through the roof, the club has also come to symbolise an identity, a statement about your geographical roots – of who you are and where you come from, wherever you may now call home.

This is why so many fathers are determined to pass the support of QPR down to their children, as Stan Bowles observed during 30 years living in west London. The tradition has to live on within families.

For the current generation of supporters, I have one wish above all others – that the club can wear a smile again during the coming season. I'm tired of tabloid speculation about who said what to whom. I want the headlines to be about what's happening *on* the pitch for a change.

But then this is QPR we're talking about. Just about anything is possible. And anyway, who am I kidding? Wouldn't we all be just a little bit bored if there wasn't a soap-opera twist or two to gossip about in the Springbok?

So back on board the rollercoaster, folks. Next stop the Premiership, hopefully . . .